THE SPECTRUM OF

Music

with Related Arts

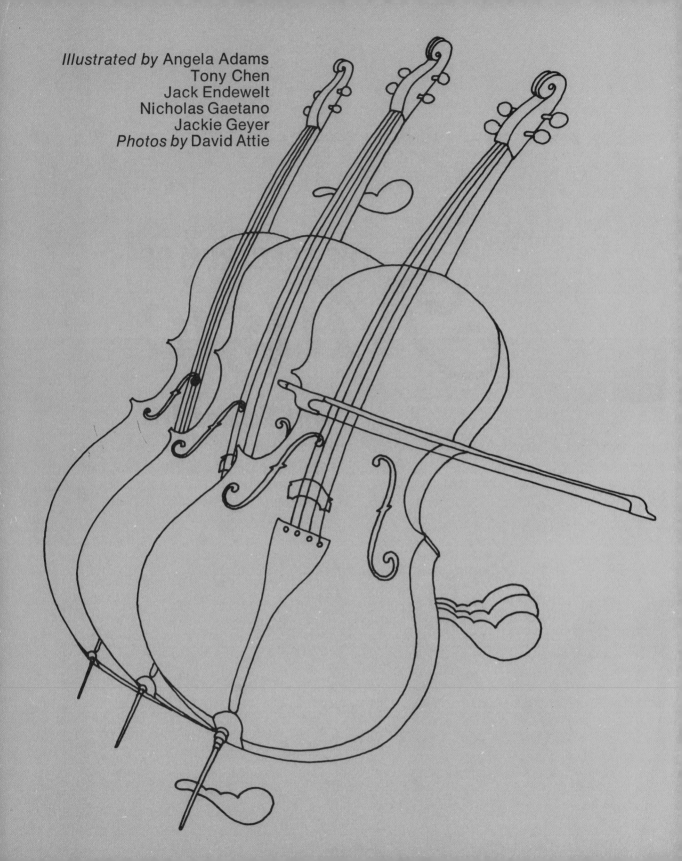

Illustrated by Angela Adams
Tony Chen
Jack Endewelt
Nicholas Gaetano
Jackie Geyer
Photos by David Attie

THE SPECTRUM OF
Music

with Related Arts

A Macmillan/Schirmer program

Mary Val Marsh
Carroll Rinehart
Edith Savage

Ralph Beelke
Ronald Silverman

Macmillan Publishing Co., Inc.
New York

Collier Macmillan Publishers
London

ACKNOWLEDGMENTS

Grateful acknowledgment is given to the following authors and publishers:

Rowena Bennett for "The Grumbling Truck" from STORY TELLER POEMS. Used by permission.

Bowmar Records, Inc. for "Hanukah Is Here" from HOLIDAY SONGS by Rinehart and Mills, copyright 1966; for "Japanese Rain Song" from SING A SONG by Roberta McLaughlin and Lucille Wood. Used by permission.

Cooperative Recreation Service, Inc. for "Power of Song" and "Early One Morning" from WORK AND SING; for "The German Band" From SCORE, copyright 1941; for "Ingonyama" from AFRICAN SONGS; for "Sandy Land" from PLAY PARTY GAMES, copyright 1940 by Lynn Rohrbough, copyright renewed 1968. For "Tina Singu," "The Tree Frog," "The Train," "Holla Hi, Holla Ho," "The Owl and the Cuckoo," "Old Texas," "Winter Song," "Street Calls" ("Chairs to Mend"), and "Amen." Used by permission.

Crown Publishers, Inc. for "Lindy Lowe" from CHANTEYING ABOARD AMERICAN SHIPS by Frederick P. Harlow. © 1962 by Barre Publishing Co., Inc. Used by permission of Crown Publishers, Inc.

Doubleday & Company, Inc., for "The Flag Goes By" and "Thirty Days Has September" ("The Days of the Month") from POEMS EVERY CHILD SHOULD KNOW by Mary Burt. Copyright © 1904, 1907 by Doubleday, Page & Company. Reprinted by permission of Doubleday & Company, Inc.

Fideree Music Corporation and Frank Music Company, Ltd. for "Dance and Whistle," words and music by Joseph Marais. Copyright 1952 Fideree Music Corporation.

Dan Gullickson for "I-lu-vi-vik." Used by permission.

Hargail Music Press for "Aydi Bim Bam" from TUM-BALALAIKA by Schwartz and Kevess, copyright 1956.

J. B. Lippincott for "Dancing" by Eleanor Farjeon. Copyright, 1938 by Eleanor Farjeon. Renewal © 1966 by Gervase Farjeon. From the book POEMS FOR CHILDREN by Eleanor Farjeon. Copyright 1951 by Eleanor Farjeon. Reprinted by permission of J. B. Lippincott Company. David Higham Associates, Ltd. for "Dancing" from SING FOR YOUR SUPPER by Eleanor Farjeon. Used by permission.

Little Brown & Company for "Owls Talking" from FAR AND FEW by David McCord. Copyright 1952 by David McCord; for "Old Joe Jones" from TIRRA LIRRA by Laura E. Richards. Copyright 1935 by Laura E. Richards.

Edward B. Marks Music Corparation for "Star Festival" from CHILDREN'S SONGS FROM JAPAN, copyright Edward B. Marks Music Corporation. Used by permission.

MCA Inc. for "The Magic Penny" by Malvina Reynolds. © Copyright 1955, 1958 by Northern Music Co., a division of MCA Entertainment, Inc., 445 Park Avenue, New York, N.Y. Used by permission. All rights reserved.

Music Sales Corp. for "A Bicycle Built for Two" by M.V. Matthews from SING ALONG WITH HARRY WILSON, copyright 1948. Used by permission.

The New Yorker for "Catalog" by Rosalie Moore. Reprinted by permission; copyright © 1940, 1968 the New Yorker Magazine, Inc.

Novello and Co., Ltd. for the translation of "Sally, Come Join in the Dancing" from FOLK SONGS OF EUROPE by Maud Karpeles, © 1956.

Theodore Presser Company for "A Fly and a Flea" from FOLKWAYS U.S.A., Book 1, by Elie Siegmeister, copyright 1954; for "Roll the Cotton Down" from KING's BOOK OF CHANTIES by Stanton King, copyright 1918 by Oliver Ditson Company; for "The Keeper" from ONE HUNDRED ENGLISH FOLK SONGS edited by Cecil Sharp, © copyright 1916 by Oliver Ditson Company. Used by permission.

G.P. Putnam's Sons for "The Greedy Cat" from TALES FROM THE FIELD by Sir George Dasent. Reprinted by permission.

G. Schirmer, Inc. for "Lullaby Carol" from THE BOTSFORD COLLECTION OF FOLKSONGS, volume 2, by Florence Hudson Botsford, copyright 1922, 1931 by G. Schirmer, Inc.; "My Bark Canoe" from THE BOTSFORD COLLECTION OF FOLKSONGS, volume 1, by Florence Hudson Botsford, copyright 1922, 1930 by G. Schirmer, Inc.; "Sugarbush" from SONGS FROM THE VELD by Joseph Marais, copyright 1942; for "The Shoemaker" from SPANISH SONGS OF OLD CALIFORNIA by Lummis and Farwell, copyright 1923, 1951 by G. Schirmer, Inc. Used by permission.

(Continued on page 262)

AUTHORS

Mary Val Marsh has been a member of the Music Education faculty of California State University at San Diego and is well known as a workshop clinician. She has had extensive experience teaching and supervising classroom music at every level from kindergarten through graduate school and is the author of *Choruses and Carols, Here a Song, There a Song,* and *Explore and Discover Music.*

Carroll A. Rinehart, Coordinator of Elementary Music, Tucson, Arizona, has served as a consultant and workshop clinician on the Manhattanville Music Curriculum Project. He is the author of four choral collections.

Edith J. Savage, Professor of Music, California State University at San Diego, has taught and supervised classroom teachers of music at every level from kindergarten through graduate school. She is the co-author of *Teaching Children to Sing,* and co-author of *First Experience in Music,* a college text for elementary teachers.

Ralph G. Beelke, Professor of Art and Design and Head of the Art Education Department, Purdue University, was formerly the Executive Secretary, Editor, and Program Director for the National Art Education Association. He has written many articles on art education for national art journals and bulletins.

Ronald H. Silverman, Professor of Art and Chairman of the Art Education Area, California State University at Los Angeles, is a member of the Professional Standards Committee of the National Art Education Association and the author of many articles and curriculum evaluations.

CONSULTANTS

William Brohn, consultant in rock and popular music, is a conductor, performer, and arranger in New York City.

Venoris Cates, consultant in Afro-American music, is a music supervisor in the Chicago Public Schools and has had long experience teaching music in elementary schools.

Wayne Johnson, musicology consultant, is Chairman of the Department of Music, Georgetown College, Georgetown, Ky.

Walter E. Purdy, consultant in music education, is Coordinator of Music Education, University of Houston.

John Rouillard, consultant in American Indian music, is a member of a Sioux tribe. He is in charge of the program of Indian studies, California State University at San Diego.

Jose Villarino, consultant in Mexican-American music, is an Assistant Professor of Mexican-American studies, California State University at San Diego.

David L. Wilmot, general consultant on the Teacher's Annotated Edition, is a Professor of Music Education, University of Florida at Gainesville.

Contents

RELATED ARTS

Contents

Contents

RELATED ARTS

Contents

RELATED ARTS

ix

Making music

The sounds of music are made with instruments. Your voice is an instrument. A piano is an instrument. A drum is an instrument.

There are many things that can be used to make art. Paint, paper, wood, and stone can be used to make art. Jean Arp used wood to make "Birds in an Aquarium." He painted the wood with bright colors. The bright colors and soft, curved shapes make this a happy work of art.

Voices make music

Music can be made with voices.
Voices sing songs. A song has words.
A song has a melody. What song
do you like best?

Singing can help you share your feelings
with other people. Sometimes songs
can say things better than words alone.

The Magic Penny

Words and music by
Malvina Reynolds

Love is some-thing if you give it a-way, give it a-way,

give it a-way; Love is some-thing if you give it a-way,

Fine

you end up hav-ing more. It's just like a mag-ic pen-ny,

hold it tight and you won't have an - y;

Lend it, spend it and you'll have so man-y

D.C. al Fine

they'll roll all o - ver the floor, for

3

Why is this music called
"The Power of Song"?

The Power of Song

Estonian Folk Song
Translation by Freda Abrams
Last Verse Adapted

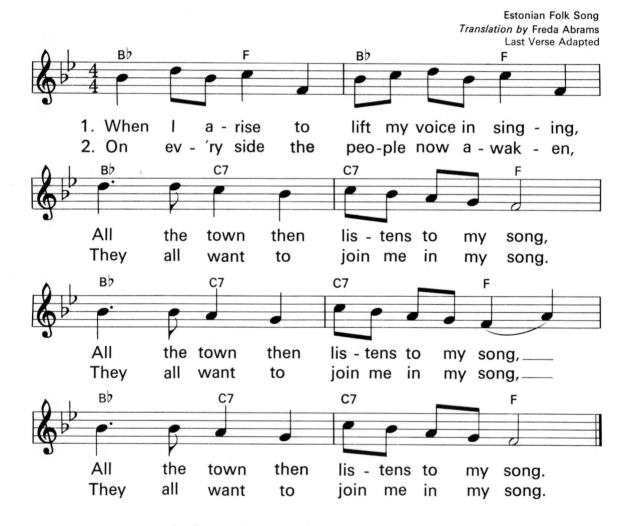

1. When I a - rise to lift my voice in sing - ing,
2. On ev - 'ry side the peo-ple now a - wak - en,

All the town then lis - tens to my song,
They all want to join me in my song.

All the town then lis - tens to my song,___
They all want to join me in my song,___

All the town then lis - tens to my song.
They all want to join me in my song.

3. From ev'ry housetop
   To the distant meadow,
   All the world can listen to my song,
   All the world can listen to my song.

4

Some songs have unusual words.
This song is a tongue twister.

Supercalifragilisticexpialidocious

Music by Richard M. Sherman
Words by Robert B. Sherman

Sup-er - cal - i - frag-il - is - tic - ex - pi - al - i - do - cious!
Sup-er - cal - i - frag-il - is - tic - ex - pi - al - i - do - cious!

Ev - en though the sound of it is some-thing quite a - tro - cious,
Sup-er - cal - i - frag - il - is - tic - ex - pi - al - i - do - cious!

If you say it loud e-nough, you'll al - ways sound pre - co - cious.
Sup-er - cal - i - frag - il - is - tic - ex - pi - al - i - do - cious!

Sup-er - cal - i - frag - il - is - tic - ex - pi - al - i - do - cious!
Sup-er - cal - i - frag - il - is - tic - ex - pi - al - i - do - cious!

5

You can sing a story. This song
tells a story about a man called Hans.
Is Hans really a brave man?

Hans of Schnocheloch

German Folk Song
Adapted by Rudolph Goehr
Words by Leo Israel

1. Brave Hans of Schnoch-e - loch, He does-n't fear a thing:
2. Bold Hans of Schnoch-e - loch, A might-y hun-ter he!

The wolf may howl, A ghost may creep,
He sees a mouse, He's up to that,

But Schnoch-e - loch is sound a - sleep.
He sends his wife to get the cat!

Brave Hans of Schnoch-e - loch, He does-n't fear a thing!
Bold Hans of Schnoch-e - loch, A might-y hun-ter he!

3. Rich Hans of Schnocheloch gets everything he needs,
But what he gets he doesn't want,
And what he wants he doesn't have,
Rich Hans of Schnocheloch gets everything he needs.

When you sing, the sound of your voice
goes up and down.

When you speak, your voice goes
up and down, too.

Make your voice go up for the question.
Make it go down for the answer.

One Day My Mother Went to the Market

Italian Folk Tune
Words by Leo Israel

One day my moth-er went to the mar-ket, And she
But when my moth-er start-ed to cook him, He did

bought a hand-some roos-ter, "A roos-ter?" "A roos-ter!"
ev-ery-thing he use-ter. "He use-ter?" "He use-ter!"

Group I   *Group II*

Oh, he said "Cock-a-doo-dle-doo, Though I love you
"Cock-a-doo-dle-doo, I must say a-

true, though I love you true." Oh, he said
dieu, I must say a-   dieu!"

Songs are sung in every language.
This song about a little donkey
is in Spanish.

Mi Burro

Words and music by
Harriet Barnett and Betty Barlow

1. Mi bu-rro es-ta can - sa-do;   ya   no an-da mas.
2. El lle - va en las ca - nas-tas   fru - tas a ven - der,

Se sien-ta en el ca - mi-no,   di - cien-do   ¡Ji - jo!
Y cuan-do yo le re - ga-ño,   con-tes - ta   ¡Ji - jo!

"Spinn, Spinn" is a German song. The song
tells of a mother who tries to make
her daughter spin thread. She promises her
new shoes and a new dress. The girl says
her finger hurts and she cannot spin.
What happens when her mother
offers to get her a husband?

8

Spinn, Spinn

German Folk Song

1. *Spinn, spinn, mei-ne lie-be Toch-ter, ich kauf dir'n Paar Schuh.*
2. *Spinn, spinn, mei-ne lie-be Toch-ter, ich kauf dir ein Kleid.*

Ach ja, mei-ne lie-be Mut-ter, auch Schnal-len da zu.
Ach ja, mei-ne lie-be Mut-ter, nicht lang und nicht weit.

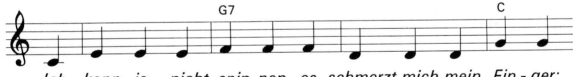

Ich kann ja nicht spin-nen, es schmerzt mich mein Fin - ger;

Und tut, und tut, und tut mir so weh.

3. *Spinn, spinn, meine liebe Tochter, ich kauf dir 'nen Mann.*
Ja, ja, meine liebe Mutter, dann streng ich mich an.
Ich kann ja schon spinnen, es schmerzt mich kein Finger;
Und tut, und tut, und tut nicht mehr weh.

9

Voices sing together

Voices sing together in
many different ways. Many voices may sing
one melody together.

One voice may sing alone. This is called
a **solo.**

One voice may sing a solo with
other voices answering. This is called
solo-response. A response is an answer sung
by a group. A singing group
is sometimes called a **chorus.**

Art can be made with things
found in nature. What things that
you find outdoors can be put
together to make art? Leaves,
stones, feathers, twigs? Look at
this picture. Name the different
objects. What can you make by
using things you find outdoors?

Solo-response songs were sung by sailors
long ago. Sailors' songs were called **chanteys.**
A chanteyman sang the solo, and the sailors
sang the response.

When you know this song, one person
can sing the solo part. The rest of the class
can be the chorus. The chorus can sing
the response.

Roll the Cotton Down

Sea Chantey

The *Lindy Lowe* was a fine ship.
She was named for a pretty girl. When you
know the song, make up some solo verses
about other girls.

Lindy Lowe

Sea Chantey

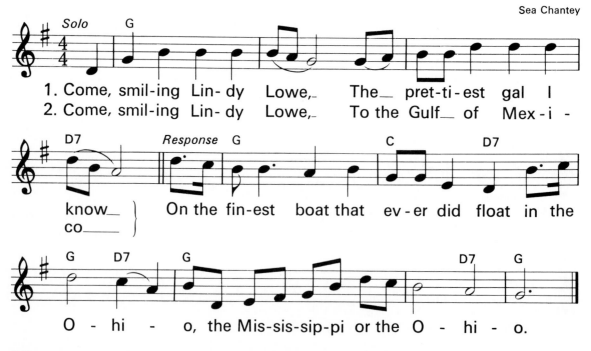

1. Come, smil-ing Lin-dy Lowe,_ The_ pret-ti-est gal I
2. Come, smil-ing Lin-dy Lowe,_ To the Gulf_ of Mex-i-

know_ } On the fin-est boat that ev-er did float in the
co____ }

O - hi - o, the Mis-sis-sip-pi or the O - hi - o.

Who Built the Ark?

Afro-American Spiritual

Who built the ark? No-ah, No-ah,

Who built the ark? Bro-ther No-ah built the ark.

Now didn't old No-ah build the ark?—
He built it long, both wide and tall,—

Built it out of a hick-o-ry bark.—
Plen-ty of room for the large— and small.

Use clay and other objects to make an ark and animals.
1. Shape an ark out of clay.
2. Collect different things, two of each kind. These pairs of things will be the "animals" for your ark. What will you use? Stones, toothpicks, beans, feathers? What else?

Several voices may sing the same melody starting at different times. This is called a **round.** "For Health and Strength" is a round.

The numbers above the music show when each group should begin to sing. When the first group gets to Number 2, the second group should begin at Number 1.

For Health and Strength

Traditional Round

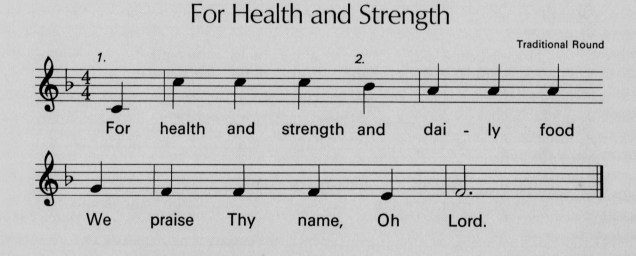

For health and strength and dai - ly food

We   praise   Thy   name,   Oh   Lord.

Play "For Health and Strength" on the bells.
One of the notes in this melody is B♭.
This sign ♭ is a **flat.**
Play the B♭ bell. Play the B bell.
What difference do you hear in these sounds?

14

"Kookaburra" may be sung as a round.

Kookaburra

Australian Round
Words by M. Sinclair

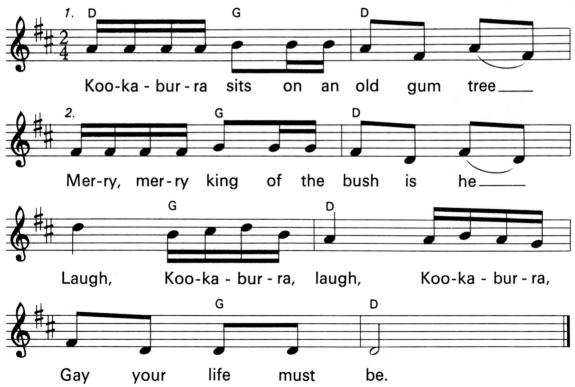

Koo-ka - bur - ra sits on an old gum tree____

Mer-ry, mer-ry king of the bush is he____

Laugh, Koo-ka - bur - ra, laugh, Koo-ka - bur - ra,

Gay your life must be.

Here is a new way to sing
"Hickory Dickory Dock." One group sings
the melody. The other group sings
a **descant.** A descant is a second part
that is sung with a melody.

Hickory Dickory Dock

Melody by J. W. Elliott
Words from Mother Goose

Hearing differences in voices

No two people look exactly alike.
No two voices sound exactly alike.
Each voice has its own special sound.
This sound is called **timbre.**

Can you hear differences in the voices
of your friends? Play this game to find out.

1. Choose someone to be the voice detective.
   She will leave the group and close her eyes.
2. Choose someone to sing the solo in the song.
   He may make up a melody to end the song.
3. Sing the whole song. Let the detective
   guess who sang the solo.

Join in the Game

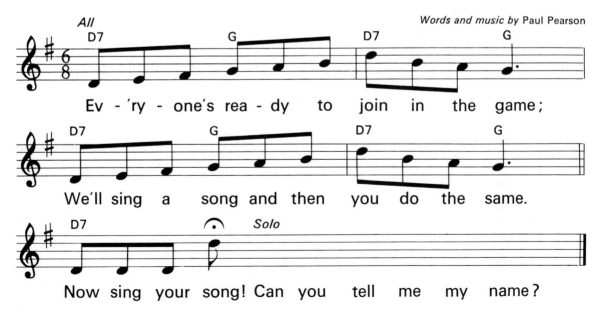

Words and music by Paul Pearson

Ev - 'ry - one's rea - dy to join in the game;

We'll sing a song and then you do the same.

Now sing your song! Can you tell me my name?

Voices of grownups have different timbres. Some women have light, high voices. These voices are called **soprano.** Some women have heavy, low voices. These voices are called **alto.** In the recording of "Hickory Dickory Dock," children sing the melody. Is the descant sung by a soprano or an alto?

Some men have light, high voices. These voices are called **tenor.** Some men have heavy, low voices. These voices are called **bass.**

LISTENING *Song of the Flea*
Modest Mussorgsky

A flea is very small. But a bass voice sings this song. This song tells a story about a happy flea. Why was the flea so happy?

Play an art detective game.
1. Place many objects in a bag.
2. Choose someone to be the detective. He will close his eyes and reach into the bag.

3. The detective will try to name what he has found by feeling it. He should tell how it feels with words such as "rough," "smooth," "soft," or "hard."

Little Jack Horner

Melody by J. W. Elliott
Words from Mother Goose

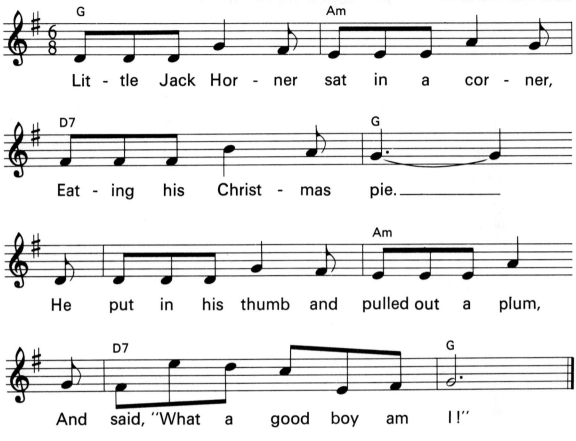

Lit - tle Jack Hor - ner sat in a cor - ner,

Eat - ing his Christ - mas pie.

He put in his thumb and pulled out a plum,

And said, "What a good boy am I!"

LISTENING *Little Jack Horner*
Michael Diack

Listen to a tenor singing the words
of "Little Jack Horner" with
a different melody. How is
the melody different?

19

When a new baby arrives, everyone
in the family thinks *this* is
the most beautiful baby ever. The mother
in this song feels the same way.

Never in Our Mountains

French Folk Song

Nev-er, nev-er   in our moun-tains was there born so sweet a

ba - by,   Such a   love - ly,   such a   pret - ty,   such a

charm-ing   lit - tle   ba - by.   Lul - la - by,   dear, while your

moth - er   tells her   pret - ty   ba - by's for - tune.

How many voices sing a **duet?**
To find out, listen to the recording.

Is the first voice in this duet
a soprano or a tenor?

20

Percussion instruments make music

The picture above shows
some **percussion instruments.**

Which ones can you name?

How are they played?

What kinds of sounds do they make?

Experimenting with sounds

The Sound-Effects Man

Mario was mad! He was so mad that he hit
the door with his fist. "**Thud!**"
What a sound! Mario hit the door again.
It made the same sound.

Mario liked the sound he had made.
He walked around the room looking for
other things to hit.

He hit the table. "**Pow!**" He hit
the wall. "**Thud!**" Mario rushed
to the kitchen. He saw lots of things
to hit. He picked up a spoon and began to tap
everything he saw.

He tapped two glasses that were
on the sink. One of them was empty,
and one had some water in it. The sounds
were different. "**Ting!**" "**Tong!**"

Mario rubbed his spoon along
a cheese grater. "**Brrrr—.**" "**Brrr—.**"

He found some metal mixing bowls
and tapped them. "**Ping! Pang! Pong!**"
"**Pong! Pang! Ping!**" "**Ping! Pong!**"

22

Just then Mario saw an egg beater
his mother had been using. He turned
the handle around and around. **"Whirrrrr—,
Whirrrrr—"** went the beater. "I like
that sound," said Mario. Then he looked at
his shirt. There was egg on it.

"Guess I should have washed
that egg beater first," he thought.

As he was thinking about his shirt,
Mario picked up a coffee can. It was
half full. He began to shake it.
"K-chu, k-chu, k-chu!" "K-chu, k-chu, k-chu!"

Then he hit the top of the can
with his hand. **"Pom——k-chu, k-chu!"**
"Pom——k-chu, k-chu!"

"I like that sound!" said Mario.

Suddenly he stopped. "We could use
that sound in our school play. We could use
lots of these sounds. Sounds could make
the play better. I could be the sound-effects man.
I could bring my own things to make
the sounds," thought Mario.

Mario couldn't wait to get to school
to tell his friends about his ideas.

Experiment with sounds the way
Mario did. Begin with things you find
in your classroom. Tap them. Scrape them.
Shake them. Listen for the sounds they make.
Look for things at home. Look in your bedroom,
in the garage, or in the kitchen.

When you find some of the sounds
Mario found, use them with
the "Song of the Kitchen."

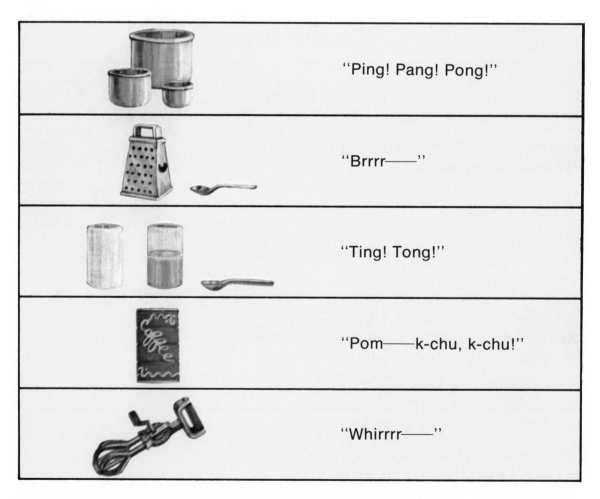

"Ping! Pang! Pong!"

"Brrrr——"

"Ting! Tong!"

"Pom——k-chu, k-chu!"

"Whirrrr——"

Song of the Kitchen

Words and music by Barbara Allen

"Ping! Pong!" "Ping! Pang! Pong!" This is the song they sing. "Brrrr,"_ "Brrrr,"_ "Ting! Tong! Ting!"

"Pom! k-chu, k-chu," "Pom! k-chu, k-chu!"

"Whirr," "Whirr," "Whirr!" "Ping! Pong!" "Brrrr!"_

"Ting! Tong!" "Whirr!" Hear the kit-chen ring!

Rondino
Warren Benson

What instruments do you hear
in this music?

Make a composition of your own using
the instruments you heard. Use this plan
for your composition.

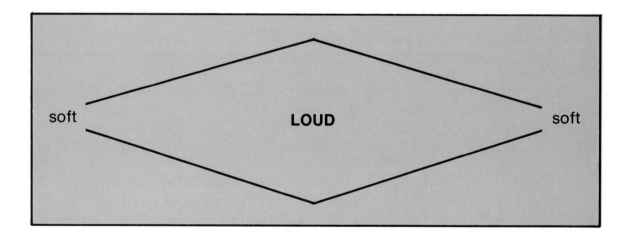

Create other music using
the same instruments. Draw a plan
of one of your compositions. The plan
will help you to remember your music.

Divide the class into two groups.
Play your composition as a round.
Decide when the second group will begin
to play.

26

Your body can be a percussion instrument.

Clap your hands.

Slap your chest.

Click your tongue.

Make other body-percussion sounds.

African people often use
body-percussion sounds as they sing.
Clap your hands and slap your legs
as you sing "Tina Singu."

The words of this song mean
"We are the burning fire."

Tina Singu

African Song

Leader Ti - na sing - u le - lu - vu - tae - o. Group Wat-sha, wat-sha,

wat-sha, Leader Ti - na, Ti - na sing - u le - lu - vu - tae - o.

Group wat-sha, wat-sha, 1. wat-sha, 2. wat-sha.

Exploring the castanets

These percussion instruments
are called **castanets.** They are made of wood.
When they are played, they make a short,
clicking sound. Experiment with the castanets.

Move as the castanets are played.
Move just your head. Move one shoulder.
Let your feet move you the way castanets sound.
Is your movement smooth or jerky?

Look at the painting "El Jaleo."
The dancer in the picture is playing
castanets. This painting has dark
parts and light parts. Where do you
see light colors? Where do you see
dark colors?

28

Castanets and tambourines are often played with Mexican music. Use these instruments as you sing and dance "Jarabe Tapatio."

Jarabe Tapatio

Mexican Folk Tune
Words by Elizabeth Evans

Why don't you meet me at the mar - ket place! ___

Why don't you meet me at the mar - ket place!

There will be good friends to greet, And hot *bur-

ri - tos to eat; With all the mu - sic so gay,

We'll want to sing and dance and shout "O - lé!"

*burrito – A corn or flour tortilla rolled up with beans inside.

29

La Raspa
Mexican Folk Dance

"La Raspa" is a favorite Mexican dance.
It is easy and fun to do. Listen
to the music. Then learn the dance.

DANCE DIRECTIONS
Choose a partner and join hands.
Stand with your right foot forward
to begin the dance.

Step A—Jump in place on
each strong pulse of the music.
On each hop, change the foot
that is forward. The step is:

   Jump, jump, jump (wait)

Do this step four times.

Step B—Hook right arms
with partner and skip around
each other four times.
Then clap hands four times.

   Skip, skip, skip, skip,
   Clap, clap, clap, clap.

Do this step again, hooking left arms.

Repeat **Step A**
Repeat **Step B**

What percussion instruments do you hear
in the recording of "La Raspa"?

30

The Grumbling Truck

There is a truck that rumbles by
And grumbles as he rumbles.
His packages are piled up high
And shake them off, though he may try,
There's not a crate that tumbles.

There is a truck that goes to town
And tries to bump his bundles down,
But though he sways and rocks and stumbles,
There's not a single box that tumbles.

When this same truck comes rattling back
Without a carton or a sack
He takes no trouble to be bright,
But with a feeble, blinking light
Through dusk and dark he gropes and fumbles;
And though he hasn't any load
To make him weary on the road,
He grumbles as he rumbles.

Rowena Bastin Bennett

What are some of the "sound words" in this poem?
Find sounds that fit these words. You might use:

      drums   castanets   rattles

You can almost hear the train wheels
going around as you sing "The Daily Express."
What instrument could make a sound
like this?

Click-et - y - clack,

The Daily Express

Words and music by Charles Harvey

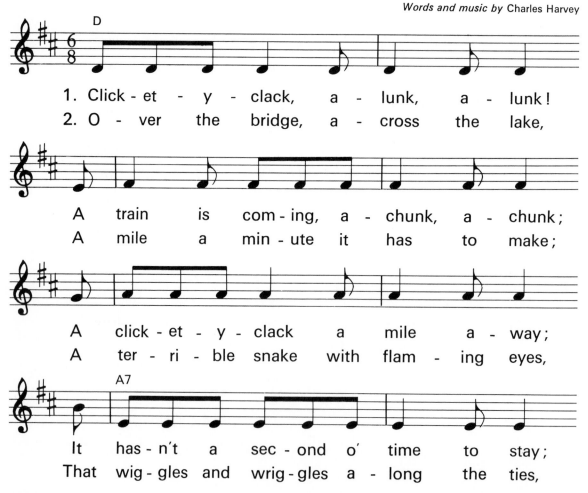

1. Click - et - y - clack,   a - lunk,   a - lunk!
2. O - ver   the   bridge,   a - cross   the   lake,

A   train   is   com - ing,   a - chunk,   a - chunk;
A   mile   a   min - ute   it   has   to   make;

A   click - et - y - clack   a   mile   a - way;
A   ter - ri - ble   snake   with   flam - ing   eyes,

It   has - n't   a   sec - ond   o'   time   to   stay;
That   wig - gles   and   wrig - gles   a - long   the   ties,

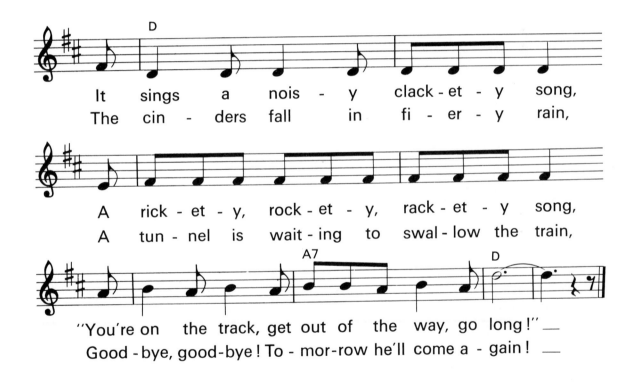

It sings a nois - y clack - et - y song,
The cin - ders fall in fi - er - y rain,

A rick - et - y, rock - et - y, rack - et - y song,
A tun - nel is wait - ing to swal - low the train,

"You're on the track, get out of the way, go long!" —
Good - bye, good-bye! To - mor-row he'll come a - gain! —

*Wood can be used to make art.
Find some small pieces of wood.
Make a train engine out of these.*

*Glue the pieces of wood together.
This is called a wood sculpture.
Paint your wood sculpture.*

Exploring the triangle

The **triangle** is made
of metal. It is played by
striking it with a metal rod.
Does the triangle make
a swishing sound or
a ringing sound? Experiment
with the triangle. Find
different ways of striking it.

TRIANGLE

Find different ways of moving
to the sounds of the triangle. Move one arm.
Move your whole body. Let your feet move you.

Play a conversation between
the castanets and the triangle. Dance
a conversation between them.

*When metal is very thin, it is easy
to bend. One kind of thin metal
is aluminum foil. Another kind is
soft wire. Experiment with pieces
of aluminum foil and soft wire.
What is the difference between foil
and wire? What kind of metal did
the artist use to make the animal in
this picture?*

How can you play the triangle
to sound like different kinds of bells?

The Ring of the Bell

Words and music by Schröder Wieck

C   G7

1. When boys are at play, and hun - gry, they say,
2. When girls are a - sleep, with dreams___ to keep,

C   G7   C   F

What are they wait-ing to hear?___ The ring of the bell
What are they hat - ing to hear?___ The ring of the bell

B♭   C   F   *(Triangle)*   G7   C

the sig - nal to tell It's time to eat!
the sig - nal to tell It's time to rise!

3. When men are at work
   And the day seems long,
   What are they waiting to hear?
   The ring of the bell, the signal to tell
   It's time to quit!

35

Have you ever been to a fair?
At a fair there are games to play,
rides to enjoy, and interesting things
to buy. What kinds of things were for sale
at the fair of Mast' Andrea?

At the Fair of Mast' Andrea

Italian Folk Song

At the fair of Mast' An-dre - a once I bought my-self a bell!

Oh, ting - a - ling, ting - a - ling, ling, a bell.

Oh, what a bar - gain, oh, what a bell!

At the fair of Mast' An-dre-a once I bought my-self a drum;

Oh, rub - a - dub, dub - a - dub, dub, a drum;

Oh, ting - a - ling, ting - a - ling, ling, a bell.

Oh, what a bar - gain, oh, what a bell!

At the fair of Mast' An-dre-a once I bought some cas-ta-nets;

Oh, click - et - y, click - et - y, cas - ta - nets;

Oh, rub - a - dub, dub - a - dub, dub, a drum;

Oh, ting - a - ling, ting - a - ling, ling a bell.

Oh, what a bar - gain, oh what a bell! ____

Play each instrument as you sing
about it in the song. Then change the words
to use other instruments.

37

Feel a metal triangle. It is hard and smooth. Metal can be used to make art.

Some metals shine. By using metal, the artist gave this sculpture a feeling of light.

38

Composing with percussion instruments

Here is a percussion picture puzzle.
Try to discover how the instruments
in each group are alike.

You can make your own
percussion composition. Find or make
some things which have interesting sounds.
These are **original instruments.**

Decide how you will group your instruments.

Draw a plan of some music for your instruments
to play. Your plan might look something
like this.

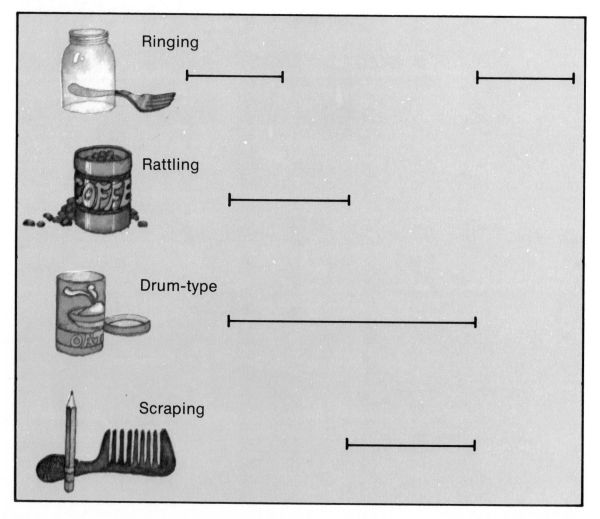

Ringing

Rattling

Drum-type

Scraping

Percussion Rondo
Danlee Mitchell

Three groups of instruments are used
in "Percussion Rondo." They are strikers,
shakers, and scrapers.

Listen to "Percussion Rondo."
Then answer these questions.

1. Which group of instruments
   is played first?
2. Which group is second?
3. Which group is third?
4. Is any group used
   more than once?

Listen to "Percussion Rondo" many times.
Draw the plan of this music.

Show the order in which the three groups
of instruments were played.

Tuned instruments
make music

Some tones are high. Some tones
are low. The highness or lowness of a tone
is called **pitch.**

Some instruments are tuned to play
many different pitches. Melodies use
different pitches. Melodies can be played
on tuned instruments.

Tuned percussion instruments

Some percussion instruments are tuned.
They can play different pitches. Which
of these instruments can you name?

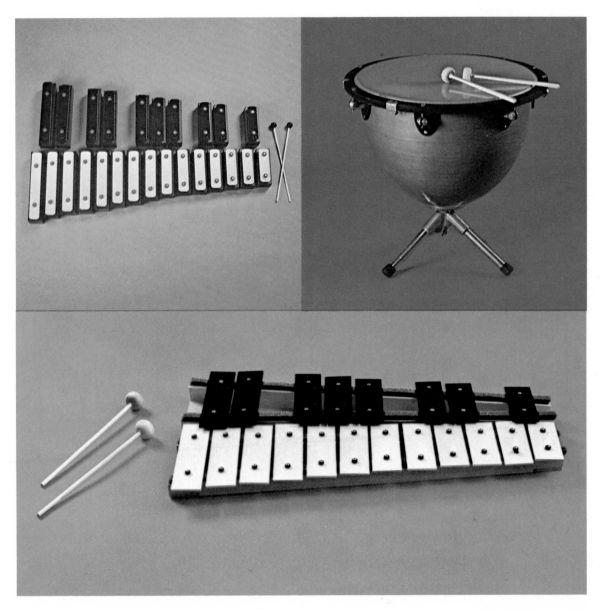

Resonator bells are
tuned percussion instruments.
Resonator bells are made in different sizes.
Each bell has a pitch.

Play a large bell. Play a small bell.
Which bell is high in pitch? Which bell
is low in pitch?

The pitches of the resonator bells
are arranged like the pitches of the piano.
Find the resonator bells that are in sets
of two and three. These bells are like
the black keys of the piano.

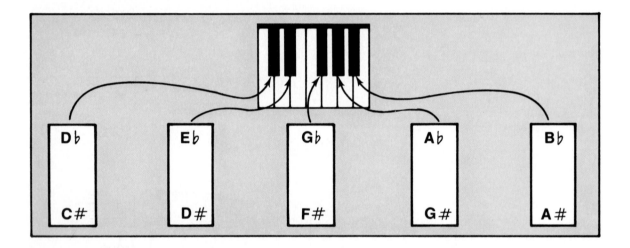

Use these black key bells to make
a tune for this poem.

> *Star in heaven*
> *What is your bright eye seeing?*
> *Winking at me!*

Make up some melody patterns on
the black key bells. Play one pattern
again and again as you sing "Star Festival."
A repeated pattern is called an **ostinato.**

Star Festival

Music *by* Kan-ichi Shimousa
Words *by* Hanayo Gondo
and Ryuha Hayashi

Finger Cymbals:

Bam - boo   leaves are   swayed by the breeze,
Sa - sa - no   ha   sa - ra - sa - ra

Stars   peep   out   a   thou - sand - fold,
No - ki - ba - ni   yu - re - ru

Glim - mer-ing bright - ly   o - ver the trees,
O - ho-shi sa - ma   ki - ra ki - ra

Stars   of   sil - ver,   stars   of   gold.
Ki - n - gi - n   su - na - go.

45

Look at the Japanese painting. The birds are sitting in a bamboo tree. Paint a picture of many bamboo leaves.

1. Use black watercolor.
2. Experiment with your brush. Fill it with black paint. Press it on your paper. Move it slowly. Lift it often.

Experiment some more. Soon you will discover many kinds of lines and shapes that look like the bamboo leaves in the picture.

You can make unusual pictures by experimenting with art materials. Paint with a brush. Paint with the edge of a piece of cardboard. Paint with a piece of cotton. Paint with a stick. How do the lines differ?

Look at this painting of school children made by a third-grade pupil. What materials do you think she used?

46

The Cover of Fog

Quietly

Words and music by Elizabeth Davis

Have you ev - er watched the fog roll
Build - ings seem to fade a - way and float in

o - ver the cit - y?____ So slow-ly, qui-et-ly, the
gray____ air.____ The cit - y slow - ly dis-ap-

1.
wet, gray fog____ cov-ers the streets and stores and cars.
pears in the soft, gray

2.
cov - er of the fog.____

This song uses only the white keys
of the piano or bells.
Find these resonator bells.
Play an ostinato as you sing
"The Cover of Fog."

47

The piano

The **piano** has black keys and white keys.
All the black and white keys make up
the piano **keyboard.** The keyboard
looks like this.

What instruments look something like
a piano keyboard?

Most piano music is made
by pressing the keys on the keyboard.
Each key moves a little hammer
inside the piano. When you strike a key,
the hammer hits a metal string.

The piano has many strings. The strings
are tuned to different pitches.

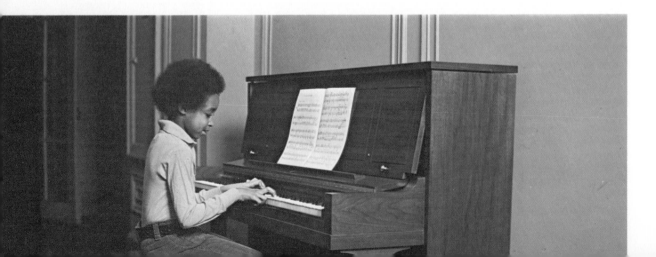

Mother, Dear Mother, I've Ripped My Boots
Béla Bartók

Listen to this piano music.
You will hear pitches that are very high
and pitches that are very low.
    How would you describe this music?
What do you hear happening?

Aeolian Harp
Henry Cowell

Some piano music sounds as though
it is being played on another instrument.
How can the piano be played to sound
like a harp?

LISTENING

Amores No. 1
John Cage

This composer has *prepared* the piano
to make unusual sounds. He has put
pieces of rubber and metal between
some of the strings. How are the sounds
of the prepared piano music different from
other piano sounds?

Stringed instruments

Stringed instruments can be tuned to play many different pitches. What stringed instruments can you name?

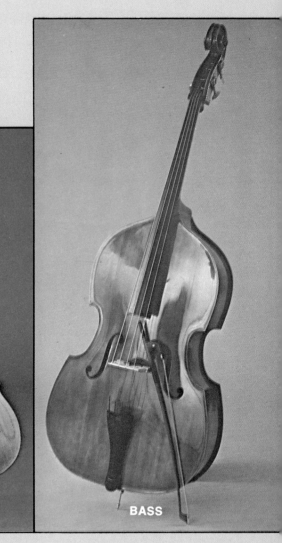

VIOLIN   VIOLA   CELLO   BASS

The autoharp

The **autoharp** is a stringed instrument.

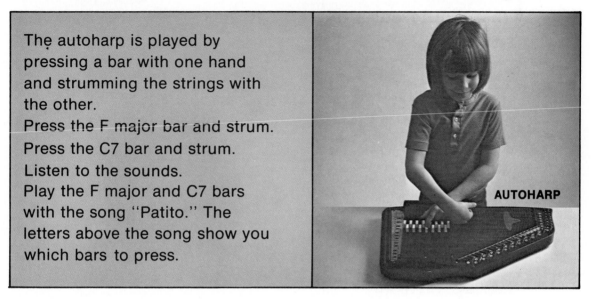

The autoharp is played by pressing a bar with one hand and strumming the strings with the other.
Press the F major bar and strum.
Press the C7 bar and strum.
Listen to the sounds.
Play the F major and C7 bars with the song "Patito." The letters above the song show you which bars to press.

AUTOHARP

Sing this song using the names of different animals. *Patito* means little duck. *Perrito* is a puppy. *Osito* is a little bear.

Patito

Mexican folk song

1. Pa - ti - to, pa - ti - to co - lor de ca - fe,
2. Me gus - ta la le - che, me gus - ta el te,

Si tu no me quier - es me quier - e Jo - sé.
Pe - ro mas me gus - tan los o - jos de u - sted.

VIOLIN

VIOLA

The viola

Another stringed instrument is the **viola.**
The viola is a little larger than the violin. It
sounds a little lower in pitch than the violin.
A viola has a more mellow timbre than the violin.

Both the violin and viola are played with a bow,
or with the fingers.

LISTENING *Sally, Come and Join the Dancing*
Portuguese Folk Song

Listen to the recording of "Sally, Come and
Join the Dancing." First you hear the viola, and
then the violin. How do the sounds differ?

52

Sally, Come and Join the Dancing

Portuguese Folk Song

Sal - ly
Fred - dy } come and join the danc-ing, Now the dance is gay and fast;

Sal - ly
Fred - dy } come and join the dancing, Now the dance is gay and fast.

If you'll on - ly be my part-ner, You shall meet me first and last;

If you'll on - ly be my part-ner, You shall meet me first and last.

STRING QUARTET NUMBER 4, Fourth Movement
Henry Cowell

Sometimes stringed instruments
are played in groups. In this music
two violins, a viola, and a cello
are having a conversation.

There are some unusual sounds
in this music for stringed instruments.
What are they? How do you think
they are made?

The first melody is played
by the violin. How many different pitches
are used in this melody?

The second melody is played by the cello.
How many different pitches are used
in this melody?

Make up your own musical conversation
on the bells or the piano.

1. Choose three pitches.
2. Ask a friend to choose
   three other pitches.
3. Play a short melody using
   your three pitches.
4. Let your friend answer,
   using his pitches.
5. Play a conversation.
6. Stop when you feel the conversation
   is finished.

BASSOON

OBOE

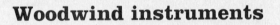

DOUBLE REED

Woodwind instruments

This large instrument is
a **bassoon.** Very low pitches
are played on the bassoon.

The **oboe** is also shown above. The oboe
sounds higher in pitch than the bassoon.

The oboe and bassoon are alike in some ways.
Both make sounds when air is blown into them
through a **double reed.** Both instruments
are members of the **woodwind family.**

56

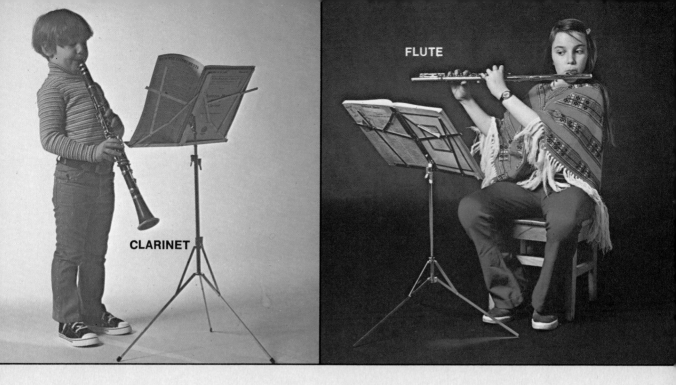

CLARINET

FLUTE

What other woodwind instruments do you know?

LISTENING *The Hen, the Donkey, and the Cuckoo*
C. Huguenin

This music is written for
three woodwind instruments. As you listen,
think about the animals that are pictured
in the music. Which animal do you hear first?
Raise your hand each time you hear the song
of the cuckoo. Listen for
the donkey's "hee-haw."

The three instruments used are
the clarinet, the oboe, and the bassoon.

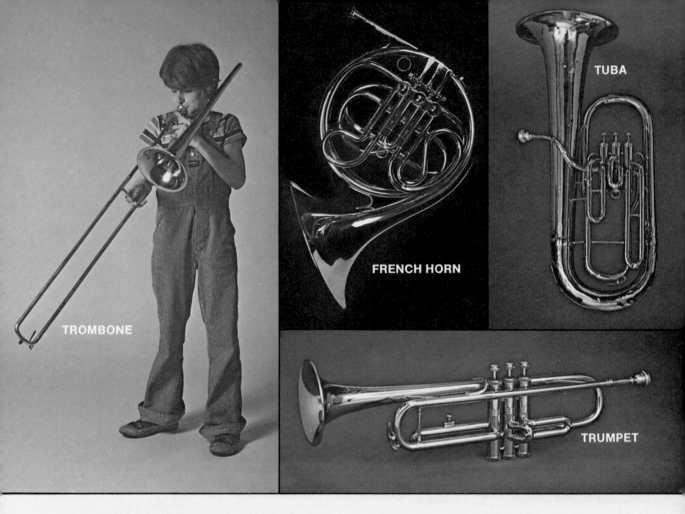

TROMBONE

FRENCH HORN

TUBA

TRUMPET

Brass instruments

The **trombone** is a brass instrument. The player moves a **slide** to change pitches on his trombone. The slide makes the trombone different from any other instrument. Sometimes it is called a **slide trombone.**

The trombone has a mouthpiece. The player buzzes his lips. The buzz makes the air in the trombone vibrate. This makes the sound. Name some other brass instruments.

58

The Purple-Eyed Pirate

There once was a purple-eyed pirate
  On the top of a tropical hill,
Who played on his tremulous trombone
  To his pedigreed parakeet, Bill.

And he played till he blew up a cyclone
  That left but a dirk and a quill
Of the picturesque purple-eyed pirate
  And his pedigreed parakeet, Bill.

Marjorie Barrows

Instruments are often played together
in a band. There are many brass and
woodwind instruments in a band. Use the names
of other instruments as you sing this song.

The German Band

Danish Folk Song
Translation by S. D. Rodholm

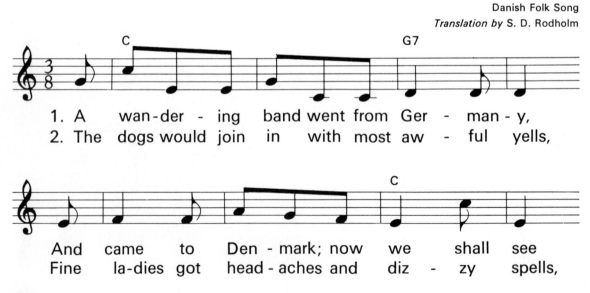

1. A wan-der - ing band went from Ger - man - y,
2. The dogs would join in with most aw - ful yells,

And came to Den - mark; now we shall see
Fine la-dies got head - aches and diz - zy spells,

What hap - pened wher - ev - er the Ger - man band
The cook left her pots and when she re - turned

went toot - ing their trom - bones in Den - mark's land.
The kit - chen was black and the steak was burned.

Refrain

Tra - la - la, la - la, la - la, la - la,

la - la, la - la - la - la - la, la - la,

Tra - la - la, la - la, la - la, la - la,

la - la, la - la - la - la - la, la - la.

3. The bookkeeper jumped and sat down again;
He made a big blot where he dropped his pen.
The grocer, confused by the German tunes,
Gave pickles to people who asked for prunes.

Fanfare in C Major
Henry Purcell

This music is played on a trombone and two trumpets. The music is a **fanfare.** A fanfare is a musical way of saying that something is about to happen.

Listen for the sounds of the trombone. It is the low-sounding instrument. When do you first hear the trombone begin to play?

Hansel and Gretel

an opera

Characters:

READER

HANSEL

GRETEL

MOTHER

FATHER

WITCH

"Hansel and Gretel" is an opera. An **opera**
is a story told in music. Voices and instruments
are used in operas. Sometimes there is
dancing too.

The music for the opera "Hansel and Gretel"
was written by Engelbert Humperdinck. He was
a German composer who lived about a hundred
years ago.

Act I

READER

In a tiny house at the edge of the forest
lived a very poor family. One day
there was no food to eat, so the mother
and father went into town to sell brooms.
The children, Hansel and Gretel, were left
at home. Hansel was told to make more
brooms. Gretel was told to knit stockings.

65

READER

As they worked, Gretel sang this
happy song.

Susie, Little Susie

Gretel

German Folk Song

Su - sie, lit - tle Su - sie, now tell me the news;

The geese are go-ing bare-foot be - cause they've no shoes.

The cob-bler has leath-er but no *last to use,

So he can-not make the poor geese their new shoes.

*last – a form that the shoemaker uses to hold the shoe while he works on it.

HANSEL

    I wish that our Mother would come back
from town.

GRETEL

    Yes, I'm so hungry I can hardly move.
I have a secret. A neighbor left
a jug and I think there may be cream
in it. Maybe Mother will make us
a pudding for supper.

HANSEL

    Cream! Oh, let's taste it. Come on,
Gretel, I don't feel like working.
Let's dance and sing a song.

Brother, Come and Dance With Me

German Folk Song
Words Adapted

Gretel

Broth-er, come and dance with me, Both my hands I give to thee,

Right foot first, left foot then, Turn a-round and back a - gain.

Hansel

Danc-ing is so new to me, I'm as clum-sy as can be;

If you'll show me what to do, I will try to dance with you.

Duet

With your feet now tap, tap, tap. With your hands now clap, clap, clap,
With your head go nick, nick, nick, With your fin - gers click, click, click,

Right foot first, left foot then, Turn a-round and back a - gain.
Right foot first, left foot then, Turn a-round and back a - gain.

The children were having so much fun that
they did not see their mother come back.
She was tired and sad because she had
not sold any brooms. When she saw the
children dancing instead of working,
she became very angry. As she began to
chase the children with one of Hansel's
brooms, she bumped against the table.
Down fell the jar of cream.

MOTHER

It's broken. What shall we eat now?
Here, take this basket, Gretel. Go out
to the woods. See if you can find
some strawberries. Hurry now! Bring
the basket back full, or you'll do
no more dancing!

READER

The children ran to the woods to hunt
strawberries. Their mother was very tired
and she fell asleep. She was awakened
by the father's singing.

Father

Tra la la la, tra la la la, Greet-ings, Moth-er, I am back!

Tra la la la, Tra la la la, Bring-ing good things in this sack!

FATHER

Look, I sold all my brooms and I have
brought many good things to eat!

MOTHER

I can't believe my eyes! Carrots,
onions, meat, butter, eggs—this is
our lucky day.

FATHER

But where are Hansel and Gretel?

MOTHER

Well, they were singing and dancing
instead of working. They caused me to spill
the cream. There was nothing
in the house to eat, so I sent them
to the woods to pick strawberries
for supper.

FATHER

Into the woods! Don't you know who lives
in there? The candy witch! She calls
children to her candy house, then bakes
them into gingerbread children.

MOTHER

Oh, no! What happens to the
gingerbread children?

FATHER

They make a good supper for the witch.

MOTHER AND FATHER

We must go at once to find our children.

Act II

READER

Hansel and Gretel went deep into
the forest. The strawberries there were
so big and juicy that Hansel ate nearly
as many as he picked.

Gretel found some wild flowers and put them
in her hair. She sang one of her
favorite songs about a flower that looks
like a little man.

There Stands a Little Man

German Folk Song
Words Adapted

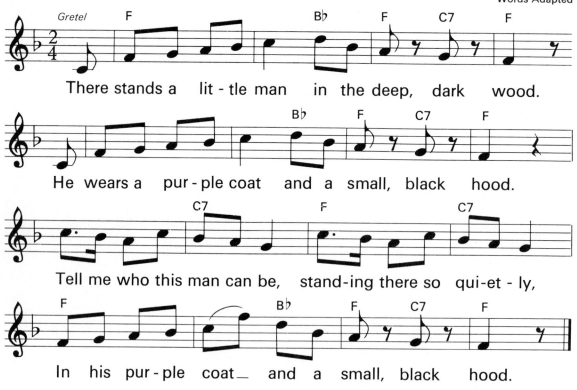

There stands a lit - tle man   in the deep, dark   wood.

He wears a   pur - ple coat   and a small, black   hood.

Tell me who this man can be,   stand-ing there so qui-et - ly,

In his pur - ple coat___ and a small, black   hood.

72

READER

It was late afternoon when the children
finally started for home. As Gretel bent
to pick up the basket of strawberries,
she gasped with surprise. The berries
had been so good that she and Hansel
had eaten them all. The basket was empty!

GRETEL

Come, we must hurry and look for more.

HANSEL

But it's too late. It's getting dark.

READER

It grew darker and darker. Hansel and
Gretel thought they saw many strange things
in the shadows. They were very frightened
and tired. They sat down and rubbed
their eyes.

HANSEL

I'm sleepy. Let's say our evening prayer.

The Children's Prayer

Words and music by
Engelbert Humperdinck

When at night I go to sleep, Four-teen an - gels watch do__ keep; Two my head are guard - ing, Two my feet are guid - ing, Two are on my right hand, Two are on my left hand, Two who warm-ly cov - er, Two who o'er me hov - er, Two to whom 'tis giv - en To light my way to Heav - - - en.

74

Act III

READER

Soon it was morning. Hansel and Gretel
woke up and looked around. They could not
believe what they saw—a beautiful house
made of candy and cake. Around the house
was a fence made of gingerbread children.

HANSEL

It's like a dream. Let's go inside.

GRETEL

Oh, we couldn't. We don't know who
lives there.

HANSEL

Well, then, let's just take a nibble.

READER

They tiptoed toward the cottage. Hansel
broke a small bite of candy from the roof.
Just as he began to eat it, a voice came
from inside the little house!

Witch

Nib-ble, nib-ble, mouse-kin, who's nib-bling at my house-kin?

HANSEL

What's that sound?

GRETEL

It's only the wind.

READER

Then Gretel became very brave, too.
She broke a tiny piece from the candy house.
But as she began to eat it, the children
again heard the voice from the house.

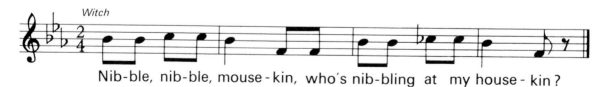

Witch

Nib-ble, nib-ble, mouse-kin, who's nib-bling at my house-kin?

READER

This time they were sure it was only
the wind, and went right on nibbling.
Suddenly Hansel felt a hand
on his shoulder.

WITCH

Won't you come inside?

HANSEL AND GRETEL

No, we can't.

READER

Then the witch sang some magic words.

Ho - cus, po - cus, witch-es spell, Do not move, I
guard you well. Back or for-ward do not go,
I have ma - gic powers, you know.

READER

The children could not move. The witch
began to build a fire in her big oven.
She was planning to bake Hansel and Gretel
into gingerbread children. The witch was
so happy that she grabbed her broomstick
and began to ride through the air.

After her ride, the witch looked into
her big oven and decided the fire was
just right.

WITCH

Come here, little girl, and test the fire.

GRETEL

But I don't know how. Can you show me?

READER

As the witch bent over the fire, Hansel
and Gretel gave her a big push and closed
the oven door.

HANSEL AND GRETEL

Hurrah! Hurrah! The witch is dead.

READER

Just then the great oven exploded.
The spell was broken. All the gingerbread
children turned back into real boys
and girls. Suddenly a familiar song was heard.

Tra la la la, tra la la la, Were_ our child-ren on - ly here!

Tra la la la, tra la la la la, Ha! Why they're real - ly here!

READER

It was their father singing. Hansel
and Gretel ran to meet their parents.
And they sang their thanks that they and
the gingerbread children were safe at last.

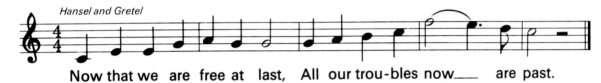

Now that we are free at last, All our trou-bles now___ are past.

The building blocks of music

Music has long and short sounds. Music has high and low sounds. The tones of music can sound together. Music can sound loud or soft, fast or slow.

A painting or sculpture is made of many shapes and colors. Look at the painting. What shapes do you see? What colors do you see?

Rhythm in music

Listen to the sounds around you.
Which sounds last a long time? Sounds
that last a long time are called
long sounds. Which sounds last a short time?
Sounds that last a short time are called
short sounds.

Look at the pictures. The things
in the pictures make sounds. Which sounds
are long? Which sounds are short?
Music is made of long and short sounds.
Long and short sounds make
the **rhythm** of music.

Play a percussion instrument.
Make a long sound on the instrument.
Make a short sound on the instrument.

Play a percussion instrument to make up
a piece of rhythm music. Making up
a piece of music is called **composing.**
Compose your rhythm piece like this.

Make some short sounds.　　－ － － － － － －

Make some long sounds.　　───　───

Make some short sounds again.　　－ － － －

Draw a picture of the rhythm
of your music.

Use your voice to make long
and short sounds. Use your voice to compose
a piece of music.

The things you see around you have many sizes and shapes. Name some that have the same shape but *different sizes. Make a drawing using shapes from nature—flowers, leaves, trees, or animals.*

83

A snail carries his house on his back.
He has a foot that goes from his head
all the way under his stomach. No wonder
he moves so slowly! If you had to carry
your house on your back,
you would move slowly, too.

The long sounds in this song
help you feel the slow movement of the snail.
A **whole note** shows a long sound. 𝅝
Find the whole notes in this song.

The Slow Little Snail

Music by Edith Savage
Words by Emilie Paulsson

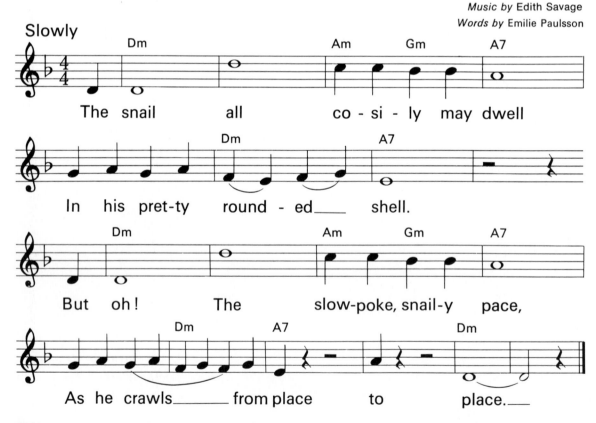

Aydi Bim Bam

Jewish Folk Song

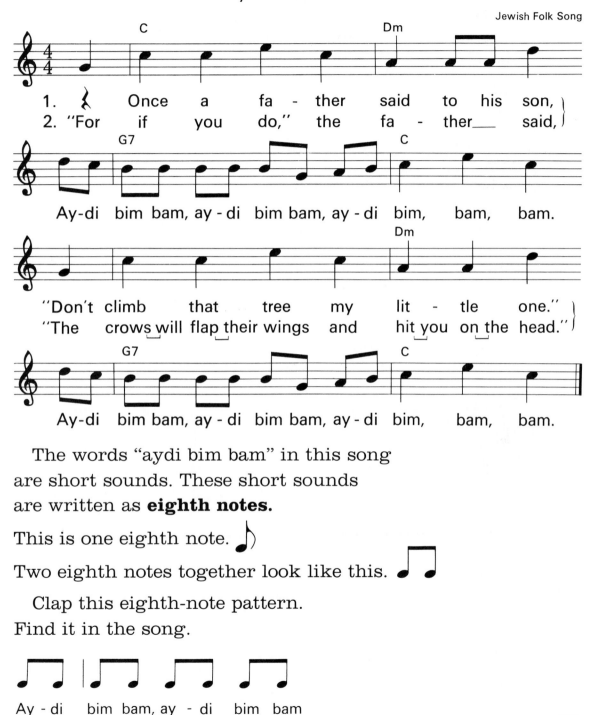

The words "aydi bim bam" in this song
are short sounds. These short sounds
are written as **eighth notes.**

This is one eighth note. ♪

Two eighth notes together look like this. ♫

Clap this eighth-note pattern.
Find it in the song.

Ay - di   bim bam, ay - di   bim bam

85

Aria
Alessandro Scarlatti

This music has long and short tones.
A flute and a clarinet play the melody.
A bassoon plays eighth notes to go
with the melody. The bassoon plays
this rhythm.

Make up a dance to go with the music.
Some of you might move to
the eighth-note pattern. Others might move
to the rhythm of the melody.

The River

The river sings
As it rushes along;
Splashing and dancing
It sings its song.

Grace Monroe

86

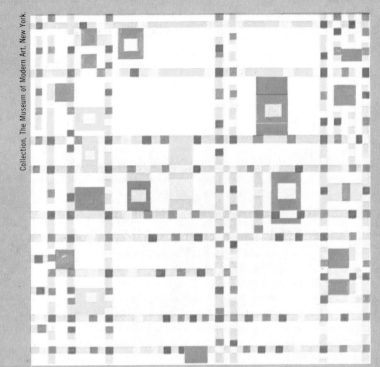

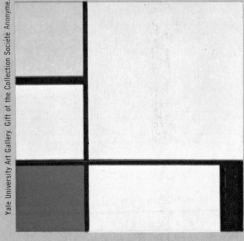

Look at the two paintings by Piet Mondrian. "Composition in a Square, 1929" is made up of a few large shapes. This picture is quiet.

"Broadway Boogie Woogie" is made up of many small shapes. Small shapes make a picture look busy.

Draw two pictures. Make one look quiet. Use a few large shapes and a few colors. Make the other picture busy. Use many small shapes and many different colors.

87

Riding a horse can be fun.
Where would you go if you had a horse
to ride?

There's a Horse

Czech Folk Song
Words Adapted

There's a horse, and of course ev-ery-bod-y knows

that you'll see al - so me ev-ery-where he goes.

Trot-ting off to dis-tant lands. Oh, how well he un-der-stands!

Such a joy, horse and boy, friend-ship ful - ler grows!

88

This is a rhythm pattern from the song "There's a Horse."

What kind of notes are these?

The other note in this pattern shows a longer sound. It is a **quarter note.**

The sound of a quarter note is twice as long as the sound of an **eighth note.**

Clap the rhythm pattern from the song. Find this pattern in the song.

In some songs there are places where you do not sing. These are called **rests.** This is a **quarter rest.** ⸜ A quarter rest lasts as long as a quarter note.

Find the quarter rests in "There's a Horse."

"Blow, Boys, Blow" is a chantey.
One sailor sings the solo. Then everybody
sings the chorus.

Blow, Boys, Blow

New England Sea Chantey

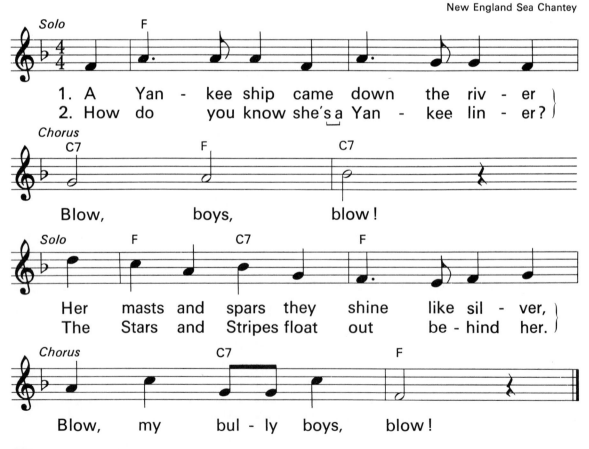

Solo   F
1. A   Yan - kee ship came down   the riv - er
2. How do   you know she's a Yan - kee lin - er?

Chorus   C7   F   C7
Blow,   boys,   blow!

Solo   F   C7   F
Her   masts and   spars they   shine   like sil - ver,
The   Stars and   Stripes float out   be - hind her.

Chorus   C7   F
Blow,   my   bul - ly boys,   blow!

What signs can you name from
this part of "Blow, Boys, Blow"?

Blow, my   bul-ly boys, blow !

This note shows a long sound. ♩
It is a **half note.** The sound of
a half note is twice as long
as the sound of a quarter note.

Find half notes in "Blow, Boys, Blow."

*Make a sculpture from pieces of
wood. Glue the sculpture to a
block of wood, or let it stand by
itself. When you have finished,
paint it. Use many colors.*

91

Clock Talk

Danish Folk Tune
Words by Mary Val Marsh

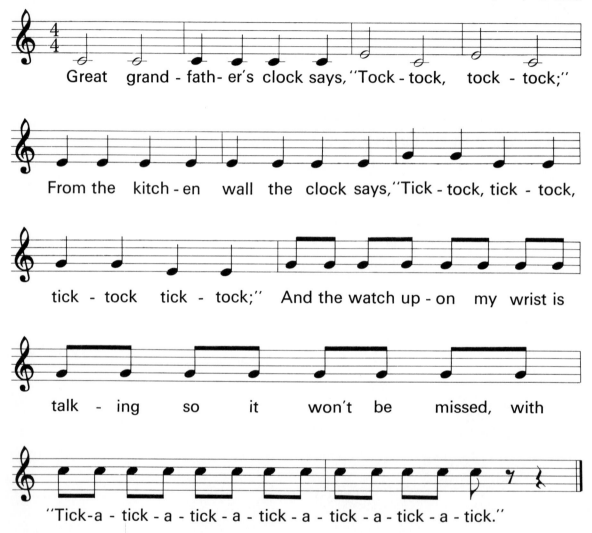

Great grand-fath-er's clock says, "Tock-tock, tock-tock;"

From the kitch-en wall the clock says, "Tick-tock, tick-tock,

tick-tock tick-tock;" And the watch up-on my wrist is

talk-ing so it won't be missed, with

"Tick-a-tick-a-tick-a-tick-a-tick-a-tick-a-tick."

How could you move to show
the different kinds of clocks in this song?
Choose instruments and movements
to accompany "Clock Talk."

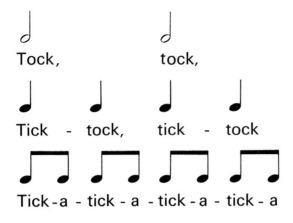

Tock, tock,

Tick - tock, tick - tock

Tick - a - tick - a - tick - a - tick - a

What kind of note is used for the sound of the
grandfather clock, kitchen clock,
wrist watch?
Make up a story about a clock shop.
Make up movements to help tell your story.
Play instruments, too.

You can cut paper so it looks like clock springs.
1. Hold a pair of scissors in one hand. Hold a square or circle of paper in your other hand.
2. Cut near the edge of your paper as you turn it.

Use different sizes and colors of paper—large, small, bright, and dull. When you have many springs, hang them up.

Making up music

Choose some instruments that
can make long and short sounds.
Put the instruments into three groups.

Have one group play this pattern.

Have another group play this pattern.

Have a different group play this pattern.

Choose a leader. A leader is called
a **conductor.** Have the conductor decide
how the patterns will be put together.

Make up some new patterns.
Choose another conductor. Make up
a different composition.

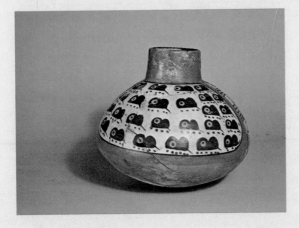

Repeated shapes, colors, and lines give a feeling of movement to art. These bowls were made by South American Indians. On one bowl, rows of mice are repeated. Your eyes move from one mouse to another. What are the repeated shapes on the other bowls?

95

"Haul Away, Joe" is another chantey.
The strong rhythm of this song
helped the sailors pull together.

As you sing "Haul Away, Joe," pretend
that you are a sailor pulling on a rope
to lift something very heavy.

Haul Away, Joe

Sea Chantey

1. A - way, haul a - way,— Come haul a - way to - geth - er,
2. A - way, haul a - way,— I'll sing to you of Nan - cy,

A - way, haul a - way,— Haul a - way, Joe.

A - way, haul a - way,— We'll haul for fin - er weath - er,
A - way, haul a - way,— She's just my style and fanc - y,

A - way, haul a - way,— We'll haul a - way, Joe.

When you sing a song, you may feel
that some tones should be stronger
than others. A strong sound in music
is an **accent.** Let the accents
of "Haul Away, Joe" help you move together.

Strum the autoharp on the accents
as you sing "Haul Away, Joe."
Play this autoharp pattern four times.

C   C | C   C | G7   G7 | C   C

Can you feel the accents?

Look at "Painting Number 5." The artist grouped many shapes together. He grouped the circles in the center of the picture. He put two circles together at the top right-hand side. Three more circles are grouped at the bottom. Find other shapes that are grouped.

This is a story about Nick and Cindy
and the sounds they hear. When you see
this sign ☆ , make sounds
that suit the story.

A Busy Day

"Hurry, Nick," said Cindy. "Let's
go play in the park."

"In a little while," said Nick.
"I'm helping Tom saw."

The saw went ZZZZ-zzzz-ZZZZ-zzzz. ☆

Cindy watched Tom saw the board.
She began moving BACK and forth,
BACK and forth with the movement of the saw.
Suddenly Tom stopped and the end of
the board dropped to the ground. ☆

"I'll race you to the swings," said Nick.
They ran as fast as they could to the park. ☆
They sat in swings.   They leaned back
and pulled on the ropes.

Nick and Cindy began to move
BACK and forth, BACK and forth,
higher and higher. ☆ Cindy began to sing.

Swing, Swing

I sing and I sing as I swing so high.

It feels as though I can touch the sky.

"Swish!" goes the wind a - gainst my face;

I feel like a bird in a high place.

Swing! Swing! Up and down. At last my feet will touch the ground.

Swing! Swing! Up and down. At last my feet will touch the ground.

Nick liked Cindy's song. He began
to sing. (Repeat "Swing, Swing.")

They jumped off the swings. ☆
Nick ran to the seesaw.

"Get on, Cindy. I'll make you
go up high."

They sat on the seesaw and held on.
Nick began to push. He and Cindy
went UP and down, UP and down. ☆
Cindy started to sing.

Up and down! Up and down! Up and down! Up and down!

Nick sang a song he knew as Cindy sang her tune.

See Saw, Marjorie Daw

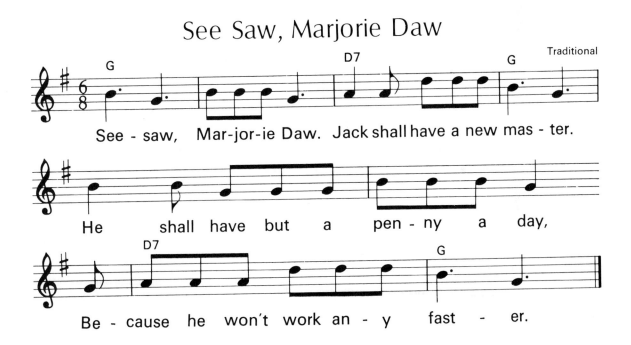

See - saw, Mar-jor-ie Daw. Jack shall have a new mas - ter.

He shall have but a pen - ny a day,

Be - cause he won't work an - y fast - er.

Suddenly there was a loud noise. ☆

"Thunder!" said Cindy.

"It's raining!" said Nick. ☆
"Let's go!" And off they ran.

"Who Did?" is a song for two groups.
Feel the accents as you sing.
Clap these accents.

Who Did?

Afro-American Spiritual

Group I G

Group II

1. Who   did?   Who   did?   Who   did?   Who   did?
2. Whale did, Whale did, Whale did, Whale did,

Who   did   swal - low   Jo - Jo - Jo - Jo?
Whale did   swal - low   Jo - Jo - Jo - Jo.

D7

Who   did?   Who   did?   Who   did?   Who   did?
Whale did, Whale did, Whale did, Whale did,

Who   did   swal - low   Jo - Jo - Jo - Jo?
Whale did   swal - low   Jo - Jo - Jo - Jo.

Who did? Who did? Who did? Who did?
Whale did, Whale did, Whale did, Whale did,

Who did swal - low Jo - Jo - Jo - Jo?
Whale did swal - low Jo - Jo - Jo - Jo.

Who did swal-low Jo - nah? Who did swal-low Jo - nah?
Whale did swal-low Jo - nah, Whale did swal-low Jo - nah.

Who did swal-low Jo -. nah down?____
Whale did swal-low Jo - nah down.____

3. Daniel, Daniel, Daniel, Daniel, } (sing three times)
   Daniel in the li-li-li-li.
   Daniel in the lion's, Daniel in the lion's,
   Daniel in the lion's den.

4. Gabriel, Gabriel, Gabriel, Gabriel, } (sing three times)
   Gabriel blow your trump, trump, trump,
   Gabriel blow your trumpet, Gabriel blow your trumpet,
   Gabriel blow your trumpet loud.

103

Discovering meter in music

Which holiday do you like best?

A Holiday Song

German Folk Song
Words by Sue Lee

Ev - ery - bod - y's sing - ing loud and clear.

It's a ver - y hap - py time of year.

Time for sing - ing just for fun,

Hol - i - days have just be - gun.

Look at the first line of
"A Holiday Song." The notes are divided
into groups by small lines.
These lines are called **bars.** | |

The bars divide the notes into **measures.**
This is a measure.

Find a measure of the song
that looks like this.

Find a measure of the song
that looks like this.

Find a measure of the song
that looks like this.

Three kinds of notes are used
in "A Holiday Song." What are they?

Clap the rhythm of the melody.

A _collage_ is a picture made of shapes cut from many different materials. Make a collage about a holiday. Cut some shapes from aluminum foil, paper, cloth, and other materials. For Christmas you could use stars, bells, and snowflakes. For Halloween you could use pumpkins, bats, and brooms. What would you use for Valentine's Day?

Cut the shapes in many different sizes. Arrange them on a sheet of paper. Try placing together two or three pieces of the same shape. Be sure to try many different groupings before you paste the pieces on cardboard.

This is a dance song from France.
Make up a dance to go with this song.
Start by making a circle. Think of
different ways to move for each verse.

Play a tambourine to accompany
this song. Play this rhythm pattern.

ONE two ONE two ONE two ONE two

Dansons la Capucine

French Dance Song
Translation by Alan Mills

1. Come, dance the Ca - pu - ci - ne, No bread, no bread have we.
1. *Dan - sons la Ca - pu - ci - ne, Y'a pas de pain chez nous.*

Al - though our neigh-bor has some, It's not for you and me.
Y'en a chez la voi - si - ne, Mais ce n'est pas pour nous.

2. Come, dance the Capucine,
   Happy and gay are we.
   Although our neighbor's weeping.
   Tears aren't for you and me.

2. *Dansons la Capucine,*
   Y'a du plaisir chez nous.
   On pleur' chez la voisine.
   On rit toujours chez nous.

Find the numbers $\frac{2}{4}$ at the beginning of the song "Dansons La Capucine."

The top number tells how many counts are in each measure. In this song there are two counts. Count, "ONE, two" for each measure.

The bottom number tells what kind of note gets one count. In this song each quarter note ♩ gets one count.

The numbers $\frac{2}{4}$ at the beginning of the song are called the **meter signature.**

Often artists will group many things together in a painting. Look at this painting "Apples and a Pot of Primroses." How did the artist group the shapes in this painting? How did the artist group the colors?

Draw some of the things you find in your classroom. Arrange the things you are going to draw on a desk or table. Group them by shape or by color. Draw or paint your grouping.

SYMPHONY NO. 7, *Second Movement (excerpt)*
Ludwig van Beethoven

A long, loud sound is heard
at the beginning of the music.
Then the first melody is heard.

As more instruments join in, the music
grows louder and louder.

Then a second melody is heard.

The music grows softer and ends quietly.

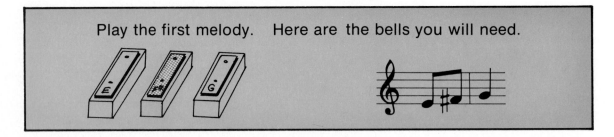

One of the tones is F♯. This sign (♯)
is a **sharp.** Find the F♯ in the melody.

What is the meter signature
of this music? How will you count
the accents of this music?

108

The meter signature of this song is $\frac{3}{4}$.
What does this tell you?

Going to Market

German Folk Song

1. O   here   is   the   po - ny   and   here   is   the   cart.
2. Now here   is   the   bas - ket   of   big   rud - dy   beets;

If   you'll   do   the   driv - ing,   then   he'll   do   his   part,
And corn,   nice and   ten - der,   that   ev - 'ry - one   eats;

I'll   sit   by your   side,   and   be   sing - ing   a   song,
We've love - ly ripe   pears with   a   blush like   a   rose,

So   take   up the   reins, let's   go   jog - ging   a - long.
And jui - cy red   ap - ples,   as   ev - 'ry - one   knows.

109

The tree frog, *el coqui*, sings a lullaby.
Would his song put you to sleep?

The Tree Frog

Puerto Rican Folk Song
Translation by Ellen George

Lit - tle   frog   from   the   tree - top   is   sing - ing,
El   co - qui,   el   co - qui a mi   me en-can - ta,

Through the   night   I   can   hear   his   sweet   song;
Es   tan   lin - do el can - tar   del   co - qui,

In   the   dark   I   can   hear   his   voice call - ing,
Por   las   no - ches   al   ir a a - cos - tar - me,

While   I'm   dream-ing   he   sings all   night long.
Me a - dor - me - ce   can - tan - do   a - si:

Co - qui!   Co - qui!   Co - qui - qui - qui - qui!

Co - qui!   Co - qui!   Co - qui - qui - qui - qui!

How are the notes and the rest
in these measures grouped?

What is the meter signature for "The Tree Frog"?
What kind of note or rest gets one count?
How many counts are in each measure?
Clap the rhythm of the melody.

This song starts with a measure
that is not complete. The notes
at the beginning $\frac{3}{4}$ ♩ ♩ | are called
pick-up notes. The song ends
with a measure that is not complete. ♩ ‖
The notes at the beginning and the note
at the end of the song
make a complete measure. $\frac{3}{4}$ ♩ ♩ ♩ |

Melody in music

A **melody** is made of different tones.
These tones can be put together in many ways.

Tones can sound very close together.

They move by steps.

Tones can sound farther apart.

They move by skips.

Some tones can sound the same.

They are **repeated tones.**

Finding skips in melody

Find this skip in "It's Great to Get Up."

It's Great to Get Up

Words and music by Michael Stevens

It's great to get   up   in the   morn - ing,   To
It's great to get   up   in the   morn - ing,   To

see   the day be - gin._____   see my friends a - gain.___ There's

plen - ty   of work   to   do this day,   And I   will do   it

just   my way.   It's great to get up in the   morn - ing,

To - day's   the   best   there's been._____

In "Wait for the Wagon" there are some big skips. One pattern with big skips looks like this.

Where do you find this pattern in the song?

Play the notes on the bells or piano.

The skip you have played is an **octave**.

Wait for the Wagon

Words and music by R. B. Buckley

Will you come with me, my Phil-lis, dear, to yon blue mountain free?
ev -'ry Sunday morning, dear, when I am by your side,

Where blos-soms smell the sweetest, Come rove a - long with
We'll jump in - to the wag-on, And all___ take a

me. It's
ride.

Wait for the wa-gon, Wait for the wa-gon,

Wait for the wag-on, And we'll all take a ride.

Knowing the staff

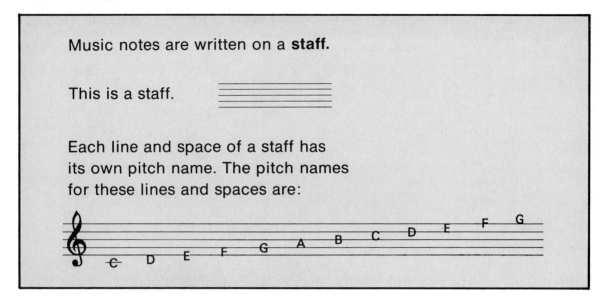

Music notes are written on a **staff.**

This is a staff.

Each line and space of a staff has its own pitch name. The pitch names for these lines and spaces are:

Have you ever thought of becoming an astronaut? Begin the countdown!

What is the name for the big skips in the first line of "Rocket to the Moon"?

What bells do you need to play the first line?

Rocket to the Moon

Words and music by Arvene Jones

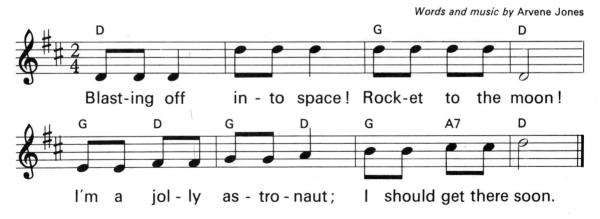

Blast-ing off in - to space! Rock-et to the moon!

I'm a jol-ly as - tro-naut; I should get there soon.

Everything in this song seems to be
out of shape. Even the tune is crooked.

There Was a Crooked Man

Traditional Music
Mother Goose Rhyme

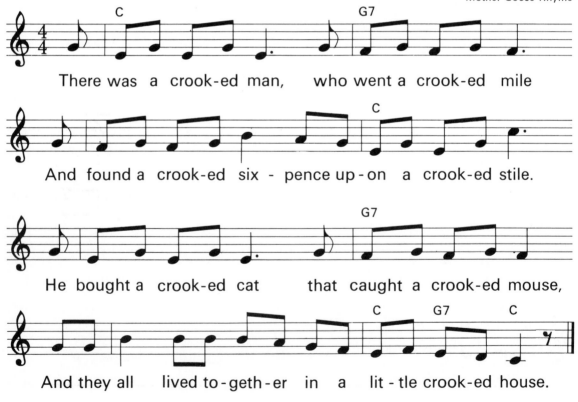

There was a crook-ed man, who went a crook-ed mile

And found a crook-ed six - pence up-on a crook-ed stile.

He bought a crook-ed cat that caught a crook-ed mouse,

And they all lived to-geth-er in a lit-tle crook-ed house.

Which lines of "There Was a Crooked Man" can you play with these three pitches?

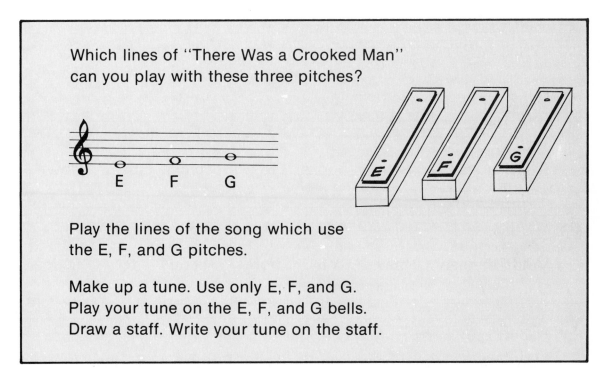

E   F   G

Play the lines of the song which use the E, F, and G pitches.

Make up a tune. Use only E, F, and G.
Play your tune on the E, F, and G bells.
Draw a staff. Write your tune on the staff.

Finding scales in melody

Boys and girls in England sang this song
many years ago. The London Bridge
in this song has been moved to Arizona.

St. Paul's Steeple

Traditional English Folk Song

Up - on Paul's stee - ple stands a tree,

As full of ap - ples as can be.

The lit - tle boys of Lon - don Town

They run with hooks to pull them down;

And then they run from hedge to hedge

Un - til they come to Lon - don Bridge.

The first line of "St. Paul's Steeple"
is a **scale.** What are the letter names
of the tones in this scale?
Play the scale on the bells.

How many times do you find this scale
in the song?

There are songs which count stars.
There are songs which count elephants.
There are songs which count angels.
This song counts mosquitoes!

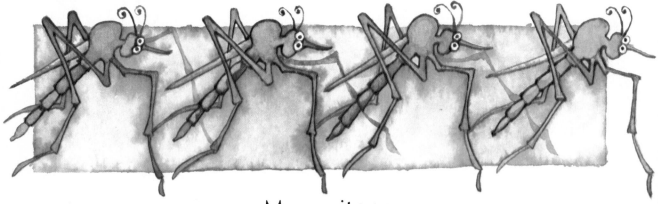

Mosquitoes

Traditional Melody
Words by Anne Morris

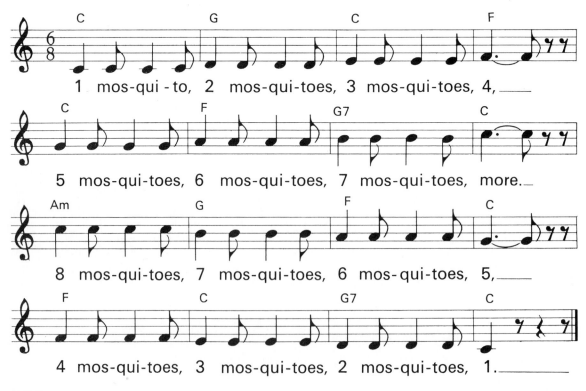

1 mos-qui-to, 2 mos-qui-toes, 3 mos-qui-toes, 4, _____

5 mos-qui-toes, 6 mos-qui-toes, 7 mos-qui-toes, more._____

8 mos-qui-toes, 7 mos-qui-toes, 6 mos-qui-toes, 5,_____

4 mos-qui-toes, 3 mos-qui-toes, 2 mos-qui-toes, 1._____

The melody of this song moves
up the scale. Then it moves
down the scale. Play the first note
of each measure on the bells. The bell part
you are playing is a scale. It is called
the C scale because the first note is C.

LISTENING
Juliet, the Little Girl
from ROMEO AND JULIET (excerpt)
Serge Prokofiev

This music describes Juliet. The music
is from a **ballet.** A ballet is a story told
through dance and music.

In part of the ballet, the music tells
about Juliet as a happy little girl.

How do the tones move at the beginning
of this music?

C D E F G A B C

Make up a dance to show
Juliet's happy feeling.

The Clown

French Folk Song
Words by Paulette Stein

Flip - pe - ty, flop - pe - ty tum - bles the clown.

I am so hap - py when he comes to town!

He wears a smile and a big, fun - ny nose,

That's why he makes peo - ple laugh, I sup - pose.

I like the flip - pe - ty, flop - pe - ty clown.

Find the place in "The Clown"
where the melody moves down the scale.
Which notes begin the scale?

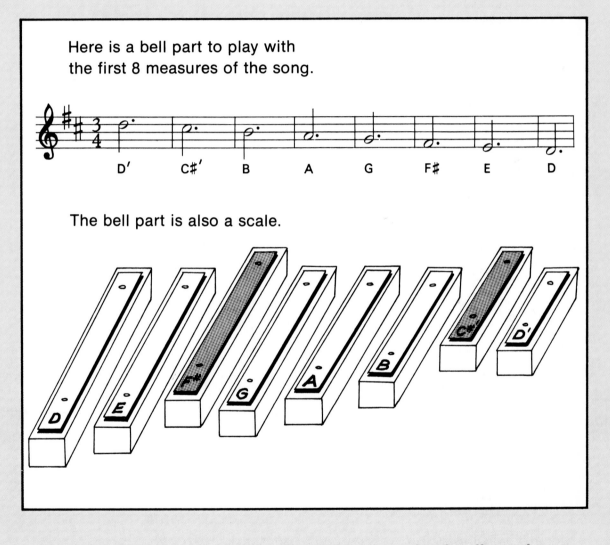

Here is a bell part to play with
the first 8 measures of the song.

D' C#' B A G F# E D

The bell part is also a scale.

*Use crayons to draw a picture
of a clown. Make your picture
happy like the song "The Clown."*

*Curved or slanting lines give your
picture a feeling of movement.
Will you use light or dark colors?*

Finding patterns in melody

The tones of a melody are grouped
into **patterns.** This is a pattern.

3   2   1

Play this pattern on the bells.

The melody pattern above is made of
rhythm and pitch. What kinds of notes make
the rhythm? What are the letter names
of the notes?

Think of a song that begins with
this melody pattern. Find this pattern in
"There Was a Crooked Man" on page 116.

Me

If I had my choice of what I'd like to be,
I wouldn't have to stop or think, you see;
I wouldn't be an elephant, a kangaroo or flea,
The only thing I want to be is me.

Alexander Williams

124

Two groups of African people argue about
whether their leader is more like a lion
or a hippopotamus. They sing the song
softly. Then they get louder and louder
as they repeat the song. They slap
their knees as they sing.

Ingonyama

Zulu Song

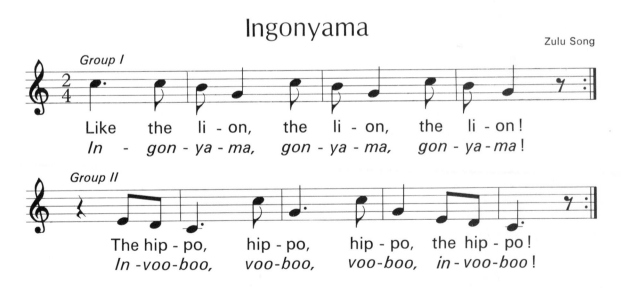

Group I

Like the li - on, the li - on, the li - on!
In - gon - ya - ma, gon - ya - ma, gon - ya - ma!

Group II

The hip - po, hip - po, hip - po, the hip - po!
In - voo - boo, voo - boo, voo - boo, in - voo - boo!

Find the E-D-C pattern in this song.
Find some other patterns in the song.

The Chinese vase gives you a pleasant feeling when you look at it. It is very graceful. Notice the curves at the top, at the neck, and top part of the body of the vase. These curves are repeated patterns.

126

Catalog
(excerpt)

Cats sleep fat and walk thin.
Cats, when they sleep, slump;
When they wake, pull in—
And where the plump's been
There's skin.
Cats walk thin.

Cats wait in a lump,
Jump in a streak.
Cats, when they jump, are sleek
As a grape slipping its skin—
They have technique.
Oh, cats don't creak.
They sneak.

Rosalie Moore

A gipsy man tells a little boy
of far-off places he has seen.

Gipsy Man

Music by Michael Stevens
Words by Dorothy King

Gip - sy man, O gip - sy man, In your yel - low car - a - van,

Up and down the world you go, Tell me all the things you know !

Sun and moon and stars are bright, Summer's green and winter's white,

And I'm the gay-est gip - sy man That rides in-side a car - a-van.

This is a pattern in "Gipsy Man."
Where do you find it in the song?
What are the pitches in this pattern?

This is another pattern in the song.
Where do you find it in the song?
What are the pitches in this pattern?

Harmony in music

Pluck two or three autoharp strings
together. Pluck two or three guitar strings
together. Play some bells together.
Play several keys on the piano
at the same time.

When tones are sung or played together
they make **harmony.** How can you
make harmony with voices?

A Visit to Grandmother

Nick and Cindy went to visit
their grandmother who lived in the country.
Each day Nick and Cindy met the mailman.
As they waited, Nick sang this song.

The Mailman

Words and music by Cynthia Gordon

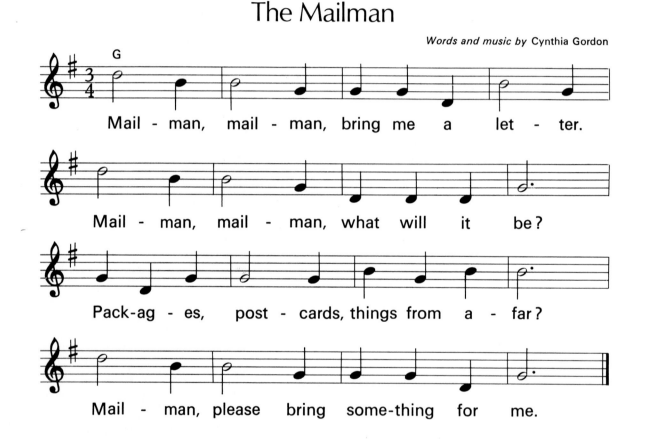

Mail - man, mail - man, bring me a let - ter.

Mail - man, mail - man, what will it be?

Pack-ag - es, post - cards, things from a - far?

Mail - man, please bring some-thing for me.

Cindy wanted to sing with him, but she started
too late. Nick had already sung "Mail-man, mail-man"
when Cindy started. They were surprised
that they could sing the song starting
at different times.

Their grandmother heard them singing.
"Why does the song sound so good?"
asked Cindy.

"Here, I will show you,"
said grandmother. She went to the piano
and played the G-B-D tones together.

Grandmother said, "This is a **chord.**
Tones that are played together make a chord.
This is the G chord. All the tones
in your song are in the G chord."

She played "The Mailman" on the G-B-D
tones at the piano.

You can play the G chord
on the autoharp while you sing the song.

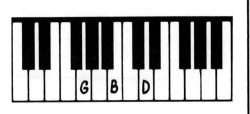

Compose a piece using all
the G, B, and D bells.

1. Make up a melody by playing
   one bell at a time.

2. Make up some music playing
   more than one bell at the same time.

3. Make your music end the way
   it began.

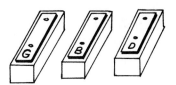

"The Mailman" can be played with
the tones of any chord. This is the F chord.

The song begins like this if the tones
of the F chord are used.

Mail - man   mail - man

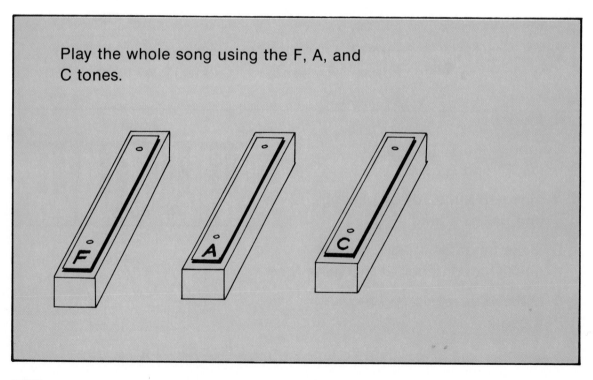

Play the whole song using the F, A, and
C tones.

Where do you find patterns that use
the tones of the F chord? Play the patterns
on the bells.

Find a scale pattern in this song.
Does it go up or down?

Early One Morning

English Folk Song

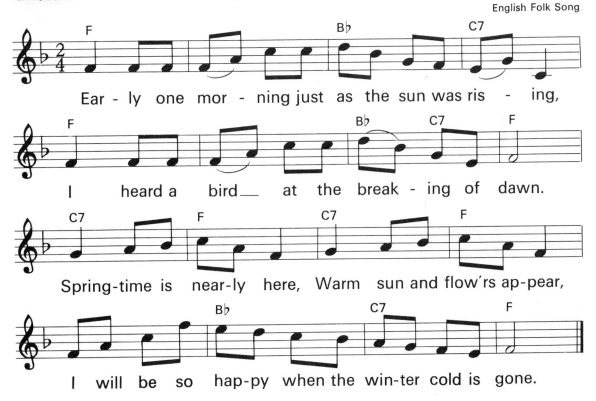

Ear - ly one mor - ning just as the sun was ris - ing,

I heard a bird __ at the break - ing of dawn.

Spring-time is near-ly here, Warm sun and flow'rs ap-pear,

I will be so hap-py when the win-ter cold is gone.

The bell part for this song has
a melody of its own. It is a descant.
Play the descant to make harmony as
you sing the song.

Which Is the Way to London Town?

Music by Carroll Rinehart
Words Anonymous

1. ♪ Which is the way to Lon - don Town?
2. And what shall I see in Lon - don Town?

O - ver the hills, a - cross the down.
Man - y a buil - ding, old and brown.

O - ver the rid - ges, o - ver the brid - ges.
Man - y a real, old fash - ioned street,_____

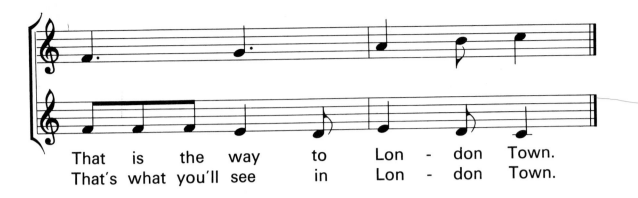

That is the way   to   Lon - don Town.
That's what you'll see   in   Lon - don Town.

Philadelphia Museum of Art. S.S. White III and Vera White Collection, Photo by A.J. Wyatt.

Shapes or colors that are the same or almost the same seem to belong together. Warm colors—orange, yellow, or red—go well together. Round and curved shapes go well together. The picture "Boat off Deer Isle" shows a sailboat on water. The blue, green, and gray colors are dark and dull. They look as if they belong together.

135

In a round the same melody is sung,
but the singers begin at different times.
This makes harmony.

"Oh, How Lovely Is the Evening"
is a round. Three groups can sing
this round. The numbers above the music
show when each group should begin singing.
Listen to the harmony when two
or three groups are singing together.
Play the last line of the song on the bells
as an introduction.

Oh, How Lovely Is the Evening

Traditional Round

1. Oh, how love-ly   is   the eve - ning, is   the eve - ning,

2. When the bells   are sweet-ly   ring - ing, sweet-ly   ring - ing,

3. Ding,   dong,   ding,   dong,   ding,   dong.

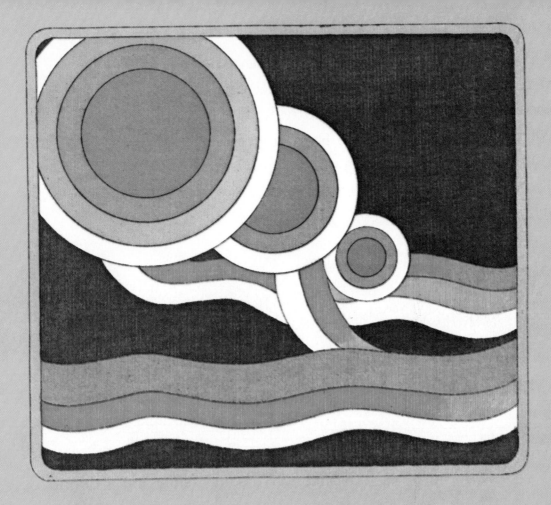

Expression in music

Words can express ideas and feelings.
Music can express ideas and feelings, too.
Soft, slow music may express
a quiet feeling.
Loud, fast music may express
a happy feeling.
Loud, slow music may express
a proud feeling.

Have you ever listened to the sounds
of night? What words would you use to tell
about night? How would you sing
a night song?

The speed of music is called **tempo.**
Should "Night Song" be sung at a slow
or fast tempo? Why?

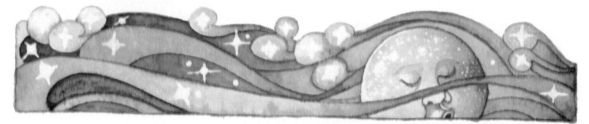

Night Song

Words and music by Elizabeth Lee Waller

Now it is night,___ stars shin - ing bright.___

Night winds are sigh - ing, soft lull - a - by - ing.

Climb in bed; rest your head.

Sounds of the night will sing you sweet dreams.

Many exciting dances move quickly.
"Krakoviak" is this kind of dance.
It has a fast tempo.

Loudness helps make music exciting.
The loudest part of this dance is marked *f*,
which stands for **forte.** Forte means loud.

The loudness or softness of music
is called **volume.**

Krakoviak

Polish Song
Words Adapted

Hand in hand danc-ing, Tra - la - la - la, la - la - la,

Back a - gain pranc-ing, Tra - la - la-la - la, la - la - la!

f

Spin a - round light-ly and clap your hands to-geth-er,

Turn a - round gai- ly, then round a-gain we go!

139

A lullaby is restful music.

At what tempo should this lullaby be sung?

Should the volume of this song
be loud or soft?

Lullaby

Basque Melody
Words by Anne Morris

Go   to   sleep,   Sand - man's call - ing, Go   to   sleep,

Close your eyes.   Dream your dreams, for an-gels will guard thee,

Dream your dreams and slum - ber on.   Go   to   sleep,

Sand-man's call - ing, Go   to   sleep,   close_ your eyes.

The Rain

Drip, drop, drip, drop,
Gently falling, falling down,
Pitter, patter, pitter, patter,
Rain is raining all around.

Splitter, splatter, splitter, splatter,
Raindrops dropping on the ground.
Splishing, splashing, splishing, splashing,
Rain is really coming down.

Dashing, smashing, splashing, crashing,
Hear the thunder's crashing sound!
Dashing, smashing, splashing, crashing,
Comes the downpour all around!

Splitter, splatter, splitter, splatter,
Gentler now the raindrops pound,
Pitter, patter, pitter, patter,
Falls the rain on field and town.

George Grimshaw

Whisper; clap hands against legs.

A little louder, with faster clapping on legs.

Voice louder; clap hands against the chest, with faster sounds.

Voices very loud; clap hands very fast against desk top.

Voices loud; clap hands against chest.

A little slower. Voices softer; clap hands on legs, getting slower and softer until coming to a complete stop.

How did the speed of the hand clapping change in "The Rain"? What do you call the fastness or slowness of sounds in music?

How did the loudness of the poem change as it was read? What do you call the loudness or softness of sounds in music?

Polka from FACADE
William Walton

A roll from the drums and the music
from the clarinets and bassoons tells you
that something is about to begin.

It is a dance, and what a funny dance!
The melody for the dance skips from
one instrument to another.

This dance has many surprises. It is
a wonderful dance for clowns! Listen to
the music. Then make a dance
with your own surprises.

National Gallery of Art, Rosenwald Collection.

This drawing is called "Circus." There are clowns in the picture. The most important clown is the one in the front. He is larger than the others. The lines of his suit are heavier and darker. This is the way the artist shows what is important. If you were to color this picture, what colors would you use?

Composing music with expression

1. Compose some clown music.
   Pick some instruments.

Plan some surprising sounds such as:

short, bright sounds   high, loud sounds

long, smooth sounds   high, soft sounds

low, quiet sounds   low, loud, booming sounds

Find a way to write your music.

Show the soft sounds with p.

Show the loud sounds with f.

Play your piece for the class.

2. Plan a composition that begins softly,
   gets loud, and then gets soft again.

This mark ($\longleftarrow$) shows that the music
is to get louder. This mark ($\longrightarrow$)
shows that the music is to get softer.
Your composition should sound like this.

$$p \longleftarrow f \longrightarrow p$$

Building music

Music is built of small parts and large parts.

There are many plans for putting parts of music together. The plan of a piece of music is called its structure.

This picture is called "The Red Studio." The artist used many different shapes in this painting. All of the shapes are grouped together to make this picture.

Putting patterns together

Small parts of music are called
patterns. Patterns are put together
in many ways to make music.
Sometimes patterns are repeated.
What melody pattern is used four times
in "Fiddle-Dee-Dee"?

Fiddle-Dee-Dee

American Folk Song

Fid - dle - dee - dee, Fid - dle - dee - dee,

The Fly has mar - ried the Bum - ble - bee.

Says the Fly, says he "Will you mar - ry me,

and live with me, sweet Bum - ble - bee?"

Fid - dle - dee - dee, Fid - dle - dee - dee,

The Fly has mar - ried the Bum - ble - bee.

This song is about a fly and a bumblebee. These are insects. Look at the pictures of insects. Which repeated shapes do you see? Paint a picture of an insect. What shapes will you use?

Street Calls

Traditional

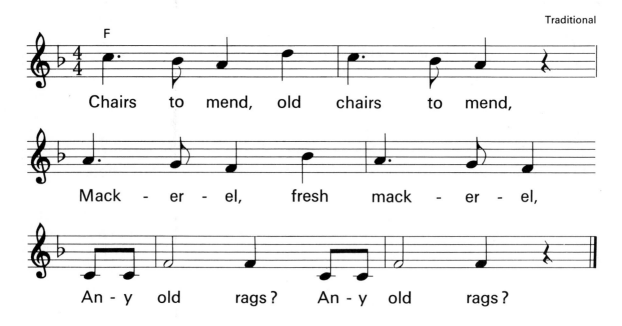

Chairs to mend, old chairs to mend,

Mack - er - el, fresh mack - er - el,

An - y old rags? An - y old rags?

What repeated melody patterns
can you find in "Street Calls"?

Old Joe Jones

Old Joe Jones and his old dog Bones;
Go jigglety-joggle over the stones;
He sells meat-pies and fishery-fries;
"Heat 'em and eat 'em!" all day he cries.
If we don't buy them, he moans and groans,
Old Joe Jones and his old dog Bones.

Laura E. Richards

148

Sugarbush

South African Melody
Adapted by Josef Marais

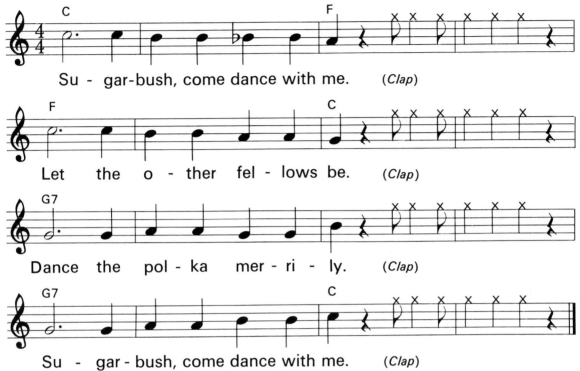

Su - gar-bush, come dance with me. *(Clap)*

Let the o - ther fel - lows be. *(Clap)*

Dance the pol - ka mer - ri - ly. *(Clap)*

Su - gar - bush, come dance with me. *(Clap)*

Notice the part of "Sugarbush" that
is clapped. This is a **rhythm pattern.** There is
another rhythm pattern in "Sugarbush."
It is the one you sang. It looks like this.

How many times do you hear
each rhythm pattern in the song?

149

Baked potatoes are good to eat.
But if they are too hot, watch out!

Baked Potato

Southern Folk Song
Words Adapted

1. Come and get your baked po - ta - to,
2. Add some but - ter, salt and pep - per,

baked po - ta - to, baked po - ta - to.
salt and pep - per, salt and pep - per.

Come and get your baked po - ta - to,
Add some but - ter, salt and pep - per,

Care - ful, it may be hot!
Care - ful, it may be hot!

How many times do you hear
this rhythm pattern in "Baked Potato"?

♩. ♪ ♩ ♩

Play the pattern on a wood block as you
sing the song.

Shapes are often repeated in art objects.   Look at the picture of   the Indian doll blanket.   What repeated shapes do you see?

Where is your favorite place for a hike?

Holla Hi, Holla Ho

German Folk Song
Words Adapted

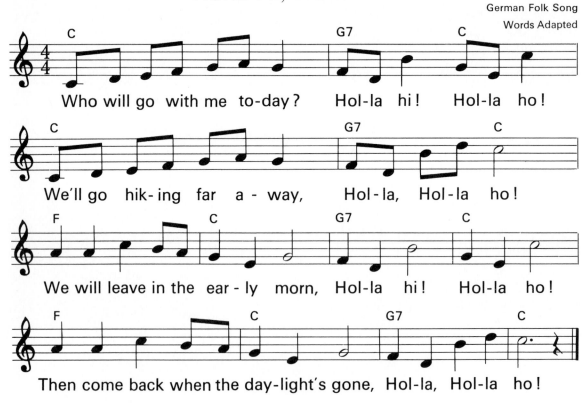

Who will go with me to-day? Hol-la hi! Hol-la ho!

We'll go hik-ing far a - way, Hol-la, Hol-la ho!

We will leave in the ear-ly morn, Hol-la hi! Hol-la ho!

Then come back when the day-light's gone, Hol-la, Hol-la ho!

Here are three melody patterns.
Play them on the bells.

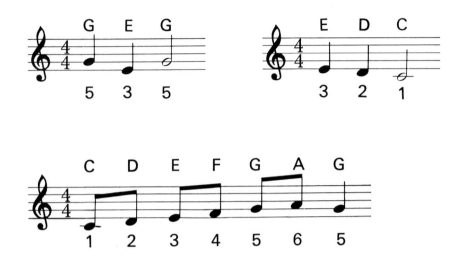

Listen to the melody patterns again.
Which of these patterns can you hear
in "Holla Hi, Holla Ho"?

The song "Holla Hi, Holla Ho" is about hiking. Paint or draw a picture about a hike you would like to take. Will your hike be in the mountains, along the seashore, or in a city park? What would you see on the hike? Trees? Birds? People? Repeat some shapes and colors in your painting. What shapes and colors have been repeated in this picture?

Here are some pitch patterns.
Play them on the bells.
Sing them with their number names.
Sing them without the bells.

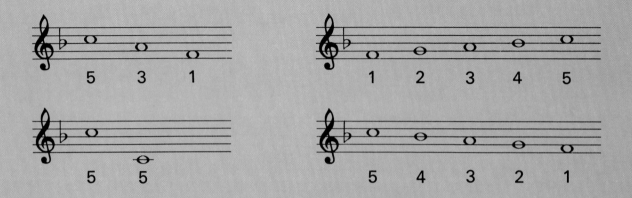

Play the patterns that move up or down
the scale. Play the octave pattern.
Play the patterns using different rhythms.

Use these patterns to build
your own melody.
Here are ways to do this.

1. Use a pattern more than once.

2. Add a pattern of your own
   for an ending.

3. Play the patterns in
   different orders.

4. Change your melody until you like
   the way it sounds.

What kind of shoes would you buy
from a shoemaker?

Which of the pitch patterns on page 154
can you hear in "The Shoemaker"?

The Shoemaker

Spanish Folk Song
Translation by Charles Lummis

I____ asked an old shoe-mak-er, Please to make me a pair of
With the toes all nice-ly rounded, Like a duck's bill__ or a

shoes - es,
goose - 's.   Con - found that old shoe - mak - er,

How he fooled me so! He made me up the shoes-es With-

out   the   duck - bill   toe.

Building with phrases

Patterns in music are put together
to make **phrases.** A phrase is a part of
a longer melody. At the end of a phrase,
the melody often seems to take a breath.

In this song the rain is falling gently.
Read the words of the song. Which words
in the song sound like rain?

As you sing, make some rain sounds
with your fingers or with an instrument.
Make your sounds soft and light like the rain.

The melody seems to breathe at the end
of each line in "Japanese Rain Song."
Each line is a phrase.

Japanese Rain Song

Japanese Folk Song
English Translation by Roberta McLaughlin

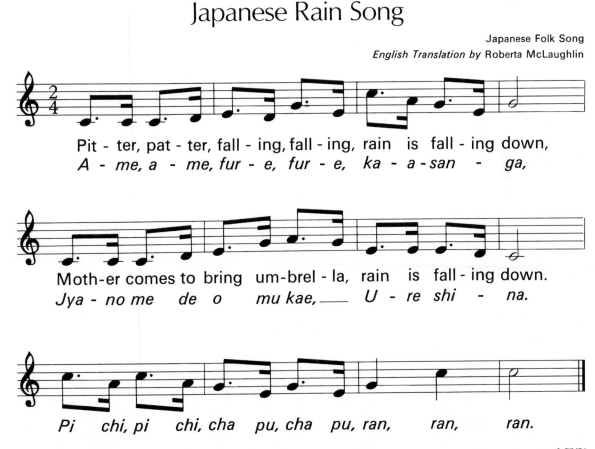

Pit - ter, pat - ter, fall - ing, fall - ing, rain is fall - ing down,
A - me, a - me, fur - e, fur - e, ka - a - san - ga,

Moth-er comes to bring um-brel - la, rain is fall - ing down.
Jya - no me de o mu kae, ____ U - re shi - na.

Pi chi, pi chi, cha pu, cha pu, ran, ran, ran.

Here are three melody patterns. Play
these patterns.

C D E F G A G

F D B

G E C

The three patterns are put together
to make a phrase. Play this phrase.

What song begins with this phrase?

Pretend that you are up in a big balloon,
sailing through the sky. Make your balloon
turn every time you start to sing
a new phrase in the song.

Up in a Balloon

English Folk Song
Words Adapted

1. Up   in a   ball-oon, boys, Up   in a   ball-oon,___
2. Blast-ing off from earth, we'll rock-et in - to   space,___

Out   a-mong the lit - tle   stars,__ sail-ing round the moon.__
All   a-long   the Mil-ky Way the plan-ets we   will chase.__

Up   in a   ball-oon, boys, Up   in a   ball-oon,___   It's
Sail - ing past a com - et   cir-cling 'round the moon.__   It's

some-thing ver - y jol-ly to be up in a   ball-oon.__
some-thing ver - y jol-ly to be fly - ing 'round the moon.

159

Curly eyes? Laughing hair? It's all
a part of Polly Wolly Doodling!

Polly Wolly Doodle

American Folk Song

1. Oh, I went down South for to see my Sal,
2. Oh, my Sal she is a———— maid - en fair,

Sing-ing Pol - ly Wol - ly Doo-dle all the day;
Sing-ing Pol - ly Wol - ly Doo-dle all the day;

My—— Sal, she is a———— spunk - y gal,
With—— cur - ly eyes and—— laugh - ing hair,

Sing-ing Pol - ly Wol - ly Doo-dle all the day.
Sing-ing Pol - ly Wol - ly Doo-dle all the day.

Fare thee well, fare thee well,

Fare thee well my fair - y fay,

For I'm goin' to Loui-si - an - a, For to see my Su-sy-an - a,

Sing-ing Pol - ly Wol - ly Doo-dle all the day.

How many phrases does this song have?
Try to sing each phrase with just one breath.

Some songs have phrases that are alike.

Listen to this song as you sing it.

Which phrases are alike?

The Train

Venezuelan Folk Song
Translation by Mary S. de Saettone

"To Ca - ra - cas," says the train, when it's com-ing from Los
"Pa' Ca - ra - cas," di - ce el tren, cuan-do vie - ne de Los

Te - ques. "To Ca - ra - cas," says the train, when it's
Te - ques. "Pa' Ca - ra - cas," di - ce el tren, cuan-do

com-ing from Los Te - ques. To Ca - ra - cas, to Ca-
vie - ne de Los Te - ques. Pa' Ca - ra - cas, pa' Ca-

ra - cas, swift - ly o - ver hills and rid - ges,
ra - cas, siem - pre lle - ni - to de gen - te

Some-times pass - ing through a tun - nel,
pa - sa a ve - ces por un tu - nel,

some - times pass - ing o - ver brid - ges.
y o - tras ve - ces por un puen - te.

Look at the picture "Manchester Valley." There is a train in this picture. The cars of the train are the same shape. Find other things with the same shape. What things are grouped together?

163

The owl and the cuckoo sing
to each other in this song.

When you know the song well,
sing both the owl's and
the cuckoo's songs at the same time.

Find two phrases in this song
that are alike. How many phrases are there
in the whole song?

The Owl and the Cuckoo

Adapted from a Dutch Folk Song

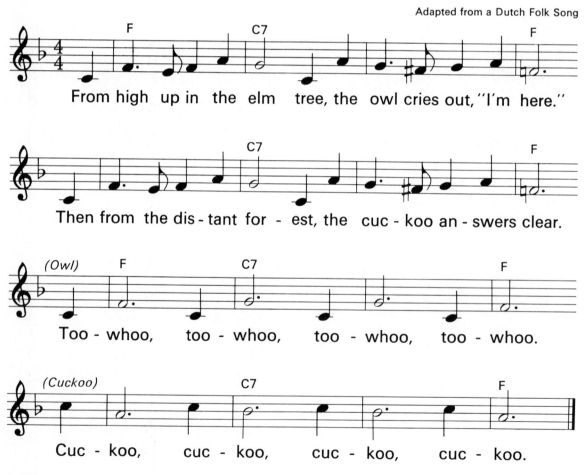

From high up in the elm tree, the owl cries out, "I'm here."

Then from the dis-tant for - est, the cuc - koo an - swers clear.

(Owl)

Too - whoo,   too - whoo,   too - whoo,   too - whoo.

(Cuckoo)

Cuc - koo,   cuc - koo,   cuc - koo,   cuc - koo.

Play this bell part when the owl sings.
Be sure to use B♭.

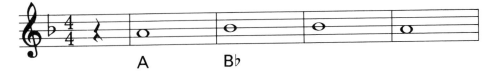

Play this bell part when the cuckoo sings.

Owls Talking

I think that many owls say **Who-o:**
At least the owls that I know do-o.
But somewhere when some owls do not-t,
Perhaps they cry **Which-h, Why-y,** *or* **What-t.**

   Or when they itch-h
   They just say **Which-h,**
   Or close one eye-e
   And try **What-t Why-y.**

David McCord

A cowboy sings this song as he plans
to leave Texas.

Play the sound of the horse's hoofs.
What instruments could you use
for this sound?

Find the two phrases in this song.

Old Texas

Cowboy Song

1. I'm going to leave___ old_ Tex-as now,___
2. They've plowed and fenced___ my_ cat-tle range,___

They've got no use___ for the long-horn cow.___
And the peo-ple there___ are_ all so strange.___

These marks are called ties.

A **tie** connects two notes of the same pitch.
A tie tells you to hold the tone as long as
the two notes would be held. Which notes
in this song are tied?

166

Winter Song

French Folk Song

Win-ter time is here, Now the wind is cold-er,

Win-ter time is here, We are one year old-er,

Frost is in the air, Birds are fly-ing south-ward,

Snow be-gins to fall, Soon we'll all go sled-ding,

Win-ter time is here, Best time of the year!

In this song, each phrase has
a curved line over it.

How many phrases are there in the song?
  Find one phrase that is <u>almost</u> like
the first phrase. How is it different?

When a group of "sweeps" gets together
to sing "Chim Chim Cheree," everyone is happy.

Chim Chim Cheree

Music by Richard M. Sherman
Words by Robert B. Sherman

Chim chim-in-ey, chim chim-in-ey, Chim chim cher-ee!

A sweep is as luck-y as luck-y can be!

Chim chim-in-ey, chim chim-in-ey, Chim chim cher-oo!

Good luck will rub off when I shake hands with you.

Or blow me a kiss and that's luck-y, too.

2. Chim chiminey, chim chiminey,
   Chim chim cheree!
   When you're with a sweep you're in glad company!
   Nowhere on earth is a happier crew
   Than those that sing Chim chim cheree, chim cheroo!
   Chim chiminey, chim chim-cheree, chim cheroo!

How many phrases are in
"Chim Chim Cheree"? Which phrases
are just alike? Find one phrase
that is unlike any other phrase.

Games with phrases

1. Here is a rhythm phrase.

    Clap the phrase or play it on
an instrument. Ask someone to play
a different rhythm phrase as an answer.

2. Here is a melody phrase.

                 1   2   3   4   5   5   4   4   3

    Play this phrase on the bells or piano.
Ask someone to play an answer, using the
same pitches in a different way.

3. Play a phrase on the black keys
   of the bells or piano.
   Ask someone to play another phrase
   on the black keys as an answer.

4. Make up a melody for this rhythm phrase.

Clap the rhythm first. Count as you clap.
Then play your melody
using any bells you wish.

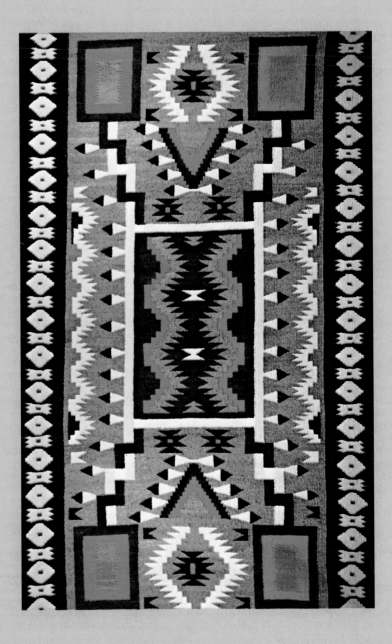

Sometimes artists and designers put shapes and colors together in a group to make a larger form. Look at the Indian rug. What are the shapes that are grouped together? Make a design for a book jacket, a rug, or wrapping paper. Group the shapes that are alike.

171

Making songs longer

This song, "Had a Little Rooster,"
gets longer with each verse.
Make the sounds of the animals
with your voice or with instruments.

Had a Little Rooster

Traditional

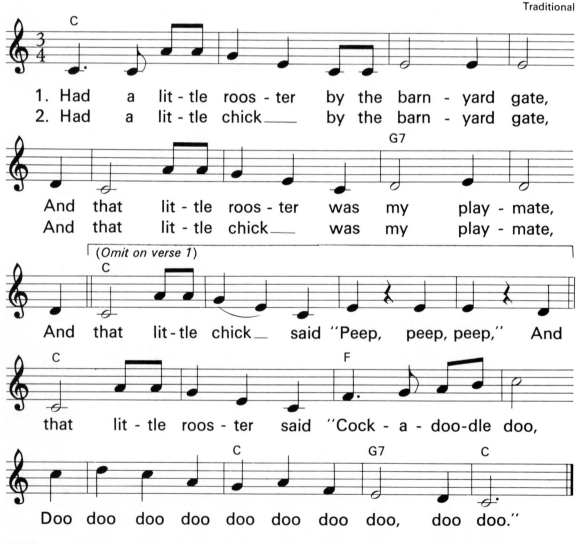

1. Had a lit - tle roos - ter by the barn - yard gate,
2. Had a lit - tle chick___ by the barn - yard gate,

And that lit - tle roos - ter was my play - mate,
And that lit - tle chick___ was my play - mate,

(Omit on verse 1)

And that lit - tle chick___ said "Peep, peep, peep," And

that lit - tle roos - ter said "Cock - a - doo-dle doo,

Doo doo doo doo doo doo doo doo, doo doo."

3. Had a little pig by the barnyard gate,
   And that little pig was my playmate.
   And that little pig said "Oink, oink, oink,"

4. Had a little duck by the barnyard gate,
   And that little duck was my playmate.
   And that little duck said "Quack, quack, quack,"

5. Had a little lamb by the barnyard gate,
   And that little lamb was my playmate.
   And that little lamb said "Baa, baa, baa."

Patterns and phrases are often repeated
to make a piece of music longer. This phrase
of "Had a Little Rooster" is repeated
for each animal you add.

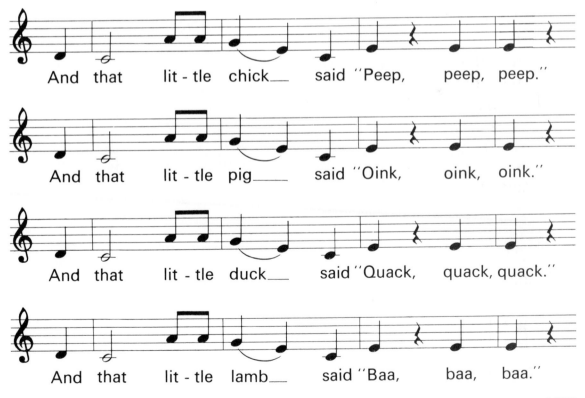

And that lit - tle chick___ said "Peep, peep, peep."

And that lit - tle pig___ said "Oink, oink, oink."

And that lit - tle duck___ said "Quack, quack, quack."

And that lit - tle lamb___ said "Baa, baa, baa."

A rhythm game

Clap this rhythm phrase.

$\frac{3}{4}$ ♩ ♩ ♩ | ♩ ♩ | ♩ ♩ ♩ | ♩ ♩ | ♩ 𝄽 |

Make the phrase longer by repeating any measure. Clap the phrase again, and repeat a different measure. Which did you like better?

You must look at a scroll on a flat table.   A few inches are unrolled at a time.   A scroll can tell a story. Make a hand scroll about "Had a Little Rooster."   It can show all the animals in the song.

Chinese artists sometimes make <u>hand scrolls</u>. The artist painted on a long roll of silk or paper. When the scroll was finished, a stick was attached to each end.   Then the picture was rolled up.

This funny song, "The Goat," gets longer
with each verse. Add some other funny verses.

The Goat

Italian Folk Song
Adapted by Rudolph Goehr
Words by Leo Israel

1. Oh, the goat came skip-ping, From the pas - ture trip-ping,

And he ate my shoe, Oh! ___ He nib-bled at my shoe,

Then he gob-bled up my shoe! What to do with just one shoe? _

2. Then a wolf came howl-ing, When the 3. And a dog came

bark-ing, When the wolf came howl-ing, When the

"The Goat"
From LITTLE FOLK SONGS. © Copyright MCMLVIII, MCMLXI, Shawnee Press, Inc., Delaware Water Gap,
Pa. 18327. International Copyright Secured. All Rights Reserved. Used by permission.

Building with imitation

Imitation is one kind of repetition. To imitate means to copy. In music, one voice or instrument can imitate another. Where do you hear imitation in the melody of "The Keeper"?

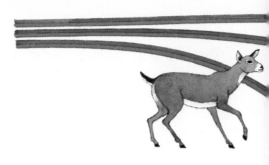

The Keeper

English Folk Song

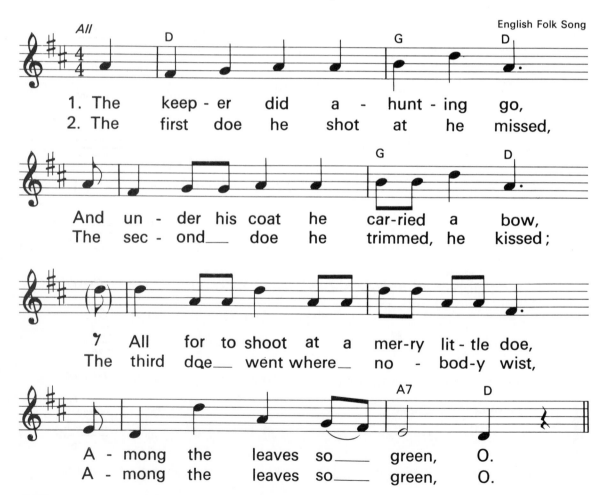

1. The keep-er did a-hunt-ing go,
2. The first doe he shot at he missed,

And un-der his coat he car-ried a bow,
The sec-ond doe he trimmed, he kissed;

All for to shoot at a mer-ry lit-tle doe,
The third doe went where no-bod-y wist,

A-mong the leaves so green, O.
A-mong the leaves so green, O.

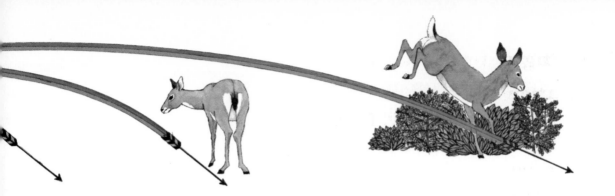

Group 1. Group 2. 1. 2.

Jack - ie boy! (*Mas - ter!*) Sing ye well? (*Ver - y well!*)

1. 2. All A7

Hey down! (*Ho down!*) Der - ry, der - ry down,

D A7 D

A - mong the leaves so___ green, O.

1. 2.

To my hey, down, down! (*To my ho, down, down!*)

1. 2. All A7

Hey down! (*Ho down!*) Der - ry, der - ry down,

D A7 D

A - mong the leaves so___ green, O.

"Amen" is a round. A round
uses imitation. One group starts a melody
and another group imitates it.
Listen for the imitation.

Amen

Afro-American Round

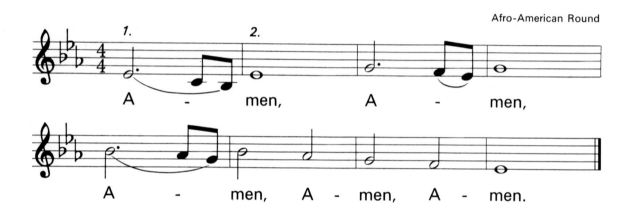

A - men, A - men,

A - men, A - men, A - men.

Clap this rhythm composition.

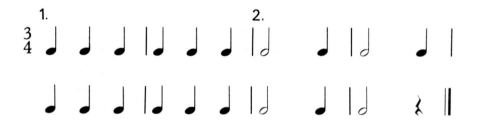

Now clap it as a round. The second group
will begin to clap at 1, when the first group
gets to 2. Listen to the imitation.

178

Wake Up

German Folk Song
Words Adapted

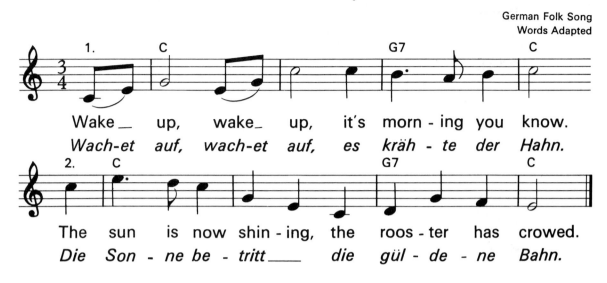

Wake __ up, wake __ up, it's morn - ing you know.
Wach-et auf, wach-et auf, es kräh - te der Hahn.

The sun is now shin - ing, the roos - ter has crowed.
Die Son - ne be - tritt __ die gül - de - ne Bahn.

When you know this song well, sing it
as a round. It is important to keep
a steady tempo when you sing a round.

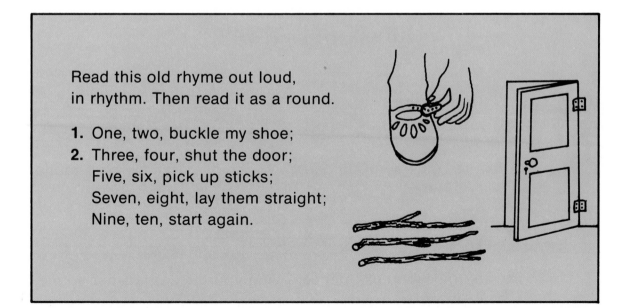

Read this old rhyme out loud,
in rhythm. Then read it as a round.

1. One, two, buckle my shoe;
2. Three, four, shut the door;
   Five, six, pick up sticks;
   Seven, eight, lay them straight;
   Nine, ten, start again.

179

Discovering musical form

The things we see or touch have shape.
We know a table by its shape. We know
a tree by its shape. Another name
for shape is **form**.

Music has shape or form. The form
of music is the plan by which its parts
are put together.

There are three parts to the song
"Dance and Whistle." Which parts are alike?

Plan a dance to show the form
of this song. Which two parts
of your dance should be alike?

Dance and Whistle

Words and music by Josef Marais

I like a (girl/boy) who can dance, swing a-round, swing a-round,

I like a (girl/boy) who can dance, swing your lit-tle part-ner round.

"Dance and Whistle"
Words and Music by Josef Marais Copyright 1952 Fideree Music Corp.
Used by permission of Fideree Music Corp. and Frank Music Co., Ltd.

181

Dancing

A hop, a skip, and off you go!
Happy heart and merry toe,
Up and down and in and out,
This way, that way, round about!

Bend like grasses in the breeze,
Wave your arms like wind-blown trees,
Dart like swallows, glide like fish,
Dance like anything you wish.

Soundless as the snowflakes white,
Swift as shooting stars at night,
Nimble as a goblin elf,
Dance, dance, and be yourself.

Stately, sprightly, so and so,
    Quick and slow,
    To and fro,
Kicking high and jumping low,
A skip, a hop, and off you go!

Eleanor Farjeon

Circus Music from THE RED PONY
Aaron Copland

Study the picture below.

Listen to "Circus Music." Listen for
this melody. Show the shape of the melody
with your hands.

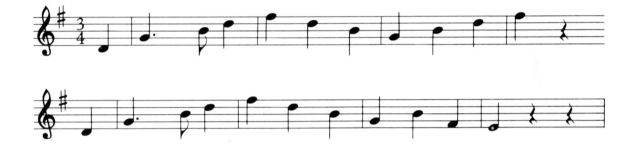

Where do you hear this melody
in the music? At the beginning?
In the middle? At the end?

How is "Circus Music" like the picture
at the bottom of the page?

*Make a hand scroll of a circus.
Use bright colors. Paint the scroll
in three parts. Draw a picture of
the ringmaster to separate each
part. The ringmaster announces
each act. Your scroll should show
the form of "Circus Music."*

Shoo, Fly

American Singing Game

A

Shoo, fly, don't both-er me, Shoo, fly, don't both-er me,

Shoo, fly, don't both-er me, For I be-long to some-bod-y.

B

I feel, I feel, I feel, I feel like a morn-ing star,

I feel, I feel, I feel, I feel like a morn-ing star. So,

A

Shoo, fly, don't both-er me, Shoo, fly, don't both-er me,

Shoo, fly, don't both-er me, For I be-long to some-bod-y.

"Shoo, Fly" is a game song.

Make up a circle dance for the
"shoo, fly" section of the song.

Choose a leader to make up something
to do for the second section.

Everyone should follow the leader. The game
will be planned like this:

[A] Circle dance   [B] Follow the leader   [A] Circle dance

 *Marche from THÉSÉE*
Jean Baptiste Lully

As you listen to this music, follow
the notes below. They show the first melody.
Listen for a repetition of this melody.

How many times did you hear the melody?

How many parts are there in this music?
Which parts are alike?

Make a picture that shows the form
of "Marche."

185

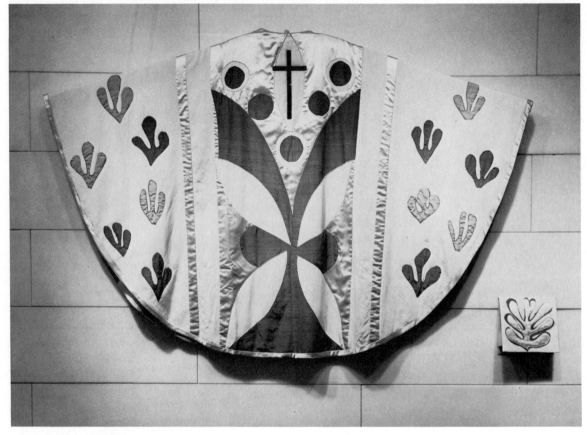

Sometimes artists and designers make things in sections. Look at the priest's robe. The robe is divided into three sections. The two side sections are almost the same. The middle section is very different. The small picture shows a design for a box cover. How many sections does it have? Which sections are the same? How is the other section different?

Make a design in sections. Decide which sections will be the same and which different.

186

Composing

Plan a composition in A B A form.
Use original instruments. Combine sounds
that are alike. Here is one plan
you might use.

A Ringing sounds   B Scraping sounds   A Ringing sounds

Try your own ideas.

Sounds of the Night

The wind whistles coldly through the trees,
Shaking the leaves in the dark of the night.
The creatures in the forest shiver and cry,
The moon casts a pale, dim light.

"Who-oo-oo," cries an owl.
"Who-oo-oo," cries an owl.
"Who-oo-oo-oo."

The wind whistles coldly through the trees,
Shaking the leaves in the dark of the night.
The creatures in the forest shiver and cry,
The moon casts a pale, dim light.

Beatrice Palmer

Composers build music in many ways

A composer may start to compose
with melodies he already knows. Which
of these melodies do you know?

Lit – tle   Bo   Peep   has   lost   her   sheep

Oh,   dear   what   can   the   mat – ter   be?

Lit – tle   Bo   Peep   has   lost   her   sheep

CHILDREN'S SYMPHONY, *Second Movement*
Harl McDonald

What familiar melodies do you hear
in this music? In what order
do you hear them?

Make a picture that shows
the form of the music.

Plan a dance that shows
the form of the music.

This is a melody you may know. Play it on the bells. Sing the song.

This melody was used in a composition by Mozart.

Mozart lived more than 200 years ago. He began to compose when he was four years old. He gave a concert when he was only six. By the time Mozart was eight, his father said he knew everything about music that a grown man should know. Mozart's music is known and loved by people in many parts of the world.

Variations on "Twinkle, Twinkle, Little Star"
"Ah, vous dirai-je, ma man"
W. A. Mozart

Listen for a familiar melody as you hear
"Variations" by Mozart. A **variation**
is a melody played in a different way.
You will hear four variations
of the familiar melody. You will need
to listen many times to find out
what happens in each variation.

How is the first variation different
from the melody you played?

In which variation is the rhythm
of the melody changed?

In which variation do you hear imitation?

Sometimes artists make several
pictures of the same thing. Each
picture may be a little different.
The differences in the pictures are
called <u>variations</u>. Look at the
drawings of a tree. Name the
variations. Draw a bug or a flower.
Then draw some variations.

Composers are always looking for ways
of making new musical sounds. A composer
may change some notes in a melody to give it
a different sound.

Here is a melody with some notes changed.
Play this melody on the bells.
How is it different from a melody you know?

E D C D E E' E D D' D E G G'

E D C D E E' E E D D' E D C'

Greeting Prelude
Igor Stravinsky

There are many kinds of greetings.
What kind of greeting is this music
bringing? Listen to find out.

192

Here is the first part of the melody of "Greeting Prelude."

How is the melody above different from the first part of the song you know?

Igor Stravinsky composed "Greeting Prelude." Stravinsky did not plan to become a composer until he was 19 years old. When he began to write music, some people liked it very much. But many people did not like it at all. It sounded very different from the music they knew. Today Stravinsky's music is often played and sung.

SUITE FOR SMALL ORCHESTRA, NO. 2
Igor Stravinsky

A **suite** is a group of short pieces
of music. There are four pieces
in this suite. Stravinsky put surprises
into each piece. Listen for the surprises.

"March"

What instruments are heard
in the introduction?
Listen for the "left-right" rhythm
in the low-sounding instruments.

"Waltz"

Would you count "ONE, two, three" or
"ONE, two, ONE, two" as you listen
to this piece?
What instrument plays much
of the high melody?

"Polka"

Is the "Oom-pah" bass rhythm heard
throughout the "Polka"?
What instruments play the melody?

"Galop"

Is the first section of the "Galop"
repeated at the end of the piece?

After you listen to this suite,
you may want to dance to it.
Show the composer's surprises
in your dancing.

A composition with improvisation

Sometimes a composer does not write down
all the music to be played. He lets
the player make up his own music.
This is called **improvising.**

Here is a composition for you to play.
You may improvise the bell part. It might
be different each time it is played.

It may help you to count
"ONE, two, THREE, four, five" as you play
the A part.

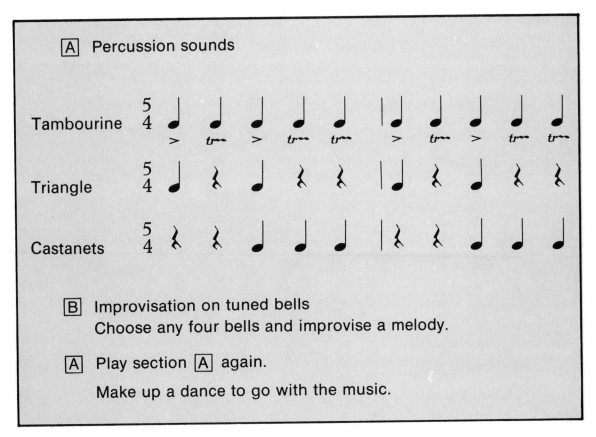

Music in our lives

Music has always been important to people. Music helps people understand each other. Songs help people tell others what they are thinking and how they feel.

"Holiday Parade" is a colorful, happy painting. The people in the painting seem to be enjoying themselves. Art can show how people feel. Art can express many different moods.

The music in our world

There is music to tell about people
and the things that are happening.
There is music to be played on new types
of instruments.

Music in our world is interesting
because it tells us about ourselves
and the people who live in our world.

198

People in many countries express
themselves through singing. There
are songs of happiness. There are songs
of sadness. Songs can also express
deep feelings. In America, people
believe in the right to go their own way.
This is called freedom.

Freedom

Words and Music by Curtis Lee

Free-dom   is   to   be   what you   want to   be,

See what you want to see,   live your life   your way.___

Free-dom is   for ev-'ry-one ev-'ry where, They have the right to share,

Free-dom   is   for   me   as well as   you!_____

Have you heard of Johnny Appleseed?
He went around the country planting
apple seeds. Many of his seeds
grew into big apple trees. The trees
made the country more beautiful.

This song is not about Johnny Appleseed.
It is about someone who would like to be
Jenny Appleseed!

Read the words of the song. Why did
the composer make up a song like this?
Why did she call it "Jenny Appleseed"?

Jenny Appleseed

Words and music by Malvina Reynolds

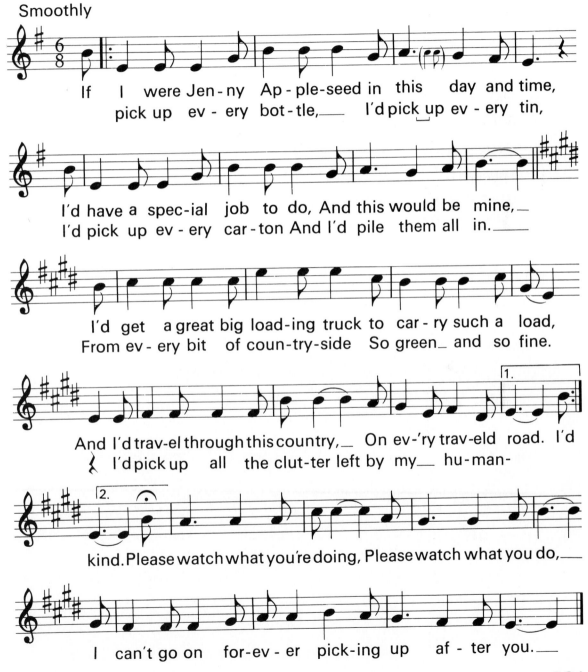

Smoothly

If I were Jen-ny Ap-ple-seed in this day and time,
pick up ev-ery bot-tle,___ I'd pick up ev-ery tin,

I'd have a spec-ial job to do, And this would be mine,___
I'd pick up ev-ery car-ton And I'd pile them all in.___

I'd get a great big load-ing truck to car-ry such a load,
From ev-ery bit of coun-try-side So green_ and so fine.

And I'd trav-el through this country,___ On ev-'ry trav-eld road. I'd
I'd pick up all the clut-ter left by my_ hu-man-

kind. Please watch what you're doing, Please watch what you do,___

I can't go on for-ev-er pick-ing up af-ter you.___

There are new sounds in today's music. Composers are changing old instruments to make different sounds. They are making new instruments. They are even using machines to make music.

LISTENING *Waltz*
Henk Badings

Many composers are working with new sounds. This composer has written a ballet using only new sounds. His ballet has five different parts. This part is called "Waltz."

Could you dance to this music?

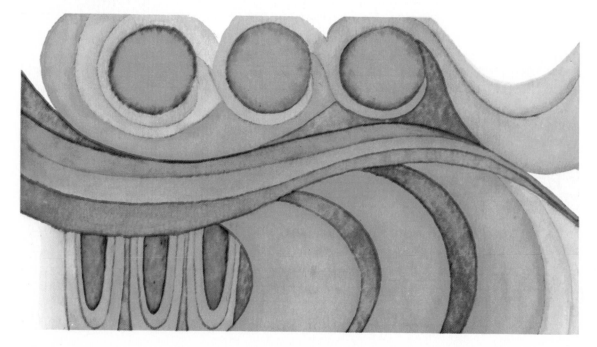

This piece of art was made with strips of aluminum. The artist painted each strip with oil paint. *As you walk past it, the shapes and colors seem to change. This is an example of today's art.*

An exciting part of today's world is
the space program. The astronauts
are helping us learn about the moon.

Space Explorer

Words and music by Archie Glenn

I think I'll go for a walk on the moon

When I get my space - ship built._____

I'll put on my hel - met and suit

And soon the earth will be far be - hind._____

For space-ships are far____ su - per - ior to cars,

Es - pe - cial - ly this one of mine._____

A Bicycle Built for Two
M. V. Matthews

Astronauts who go into space need help.
One of their most important helpers is
the computer.

As you listen to the computer's song,
you will hear a melody and
an accompaniment. It sounds like
an old piano. Listen closely. The sound
is made by a computer, and not a piano
at all.

Collection, Whitney Museum of American Art. Gift of Howard and Jean Lipman.

*Artists of today sometimes use
electricity in their art. Electric
motors may be used to move pieces
of a sculpture. Electric light bulbs
give color to a sculpture. This is a
light sculpture. Of what does this
sculpture remind you?*

Music of the first Americans

America has many kinds of new music.
But there is also some very old music
in America. Some of it
has never been written down. It
has been sung by parents to children for
hundreds of years. The Eskimo people sing
such songs. So do the Indian and
Hawaiian people.

In this Eskimo dance song the singers chant
sounds as they dance. They act out
a story about a hunter who is followed by
swarms of mosquitoes. Heavy accents
in the music tell the singers when to wave
their arms to shoo away the mosquitoes.

The Mosquito Dance

Eskimo Chant

Hai - yai   yai   yai_ yai hai   hai____ yai yai,

Hai   yai Yai_ yai   yai yai   yai yai____ yai yai yai

hai   yai yai   yai hai   yai yai   yai !

The Eskimos play a loud drum pattern
for two or three measures before they begin
to sing. They play this drum pattern for
the entire song
"The Mosquito Dance."

Sing this Indian song softly. The words
are in English so you can sing them easily.

How is this song different from
"The Mosquito Dance"?

My Bark Canoe

Ojibway Song

1. In the dark night, the long night through,
2. In the star - light, in fall - ing dew,

I guide___ my bark ca - noe,
I guide___ my bark ca - noe,

My bark ca-noe___ the long night through.
My bark ca-noe___ in fall - ing dew.

How many different tones
does this song have? The tones
in each phrase move from high to low.
This downward movement is often found
in Indian melodies.

The eagle soars
Far into the sky,
His wings spread wide
To cover the earth.
His feathers are prayers
He takes to the Great Spirit.

Indian Dance Song

Iktomi is a spider. The Indian people
tell this tale about Iktomi. Make up
some musical sounds to help tell the story.
You can use a drum, some ankle bells, and
some Indian rattles. You might find ways
to make the sounds of the wind and of
the branches rubbing together.
Choose someone for each character in the story.
Choose two readers.

A Tale of Iktomi

from a Dakota Indian legend

FIRST READER

This is a story about Iktomi, the spider.
Iktomi was tired and hungry. He sat
under a cottonwood tree to rest
before dinner.

SECOND READER

A breeze began to blow from the east.
Two branches began to rub together
just above Iktomi's head. The noise
of the rubbing grew loud.

IKTOMI

"Stop! Stop! I am tired.
I cannot rest with all this noise!"

FIRST READER

The branches paid no attention to Iktomi.
They did not stop rubbing. The wind

did not stop blowing. Iktomi became
very angry. He decided to climb the tree.
He would <u>make</u> the branches keep quiet.
So up the tree went Iktomi.

IKTOMI
   "Stop this foolish noise!"

SECOND READER
   Iktomi put his foot between the branches
   to stop their rubbing. The East Wind heard
   Iktomi's shouts and stopped blowing. The wind
   stopped so quickly that the branches stayed
   where they were. Iktomi's foot was caught
   between them. Iktomi tried and he tried,
   but he could not get away.

IKTOMI
   "Oh, tree, please help me. Please let me go!"

TREE
   "Iktomi, I cannot help you. It was
   the East Wind who made my branches rub together.
   He is playing a trick on you. We must call
   to the East Wind. Perhaps if we sing nicely,
   he will come back."

211

So the tree sang to the wind, and Iktomi sang
with the tree. Other trees nearby joined in
the song to the East Wind. This is the song
they sang:

"Wind, wind, please come back!
Iktomi is very tired and hungry!"

Children's Choir

Tah tae   tah tae   ah kae   ku yae   Tah tae   tah

tae   ah kae   ku yae   Ik - to - mi   li - la   wo - ta   chin.

212

Then the trees began to sway and to chant.
Lizards and a tortoise, and all the things
that lived on the earth joined in the chant
to the East Wind.

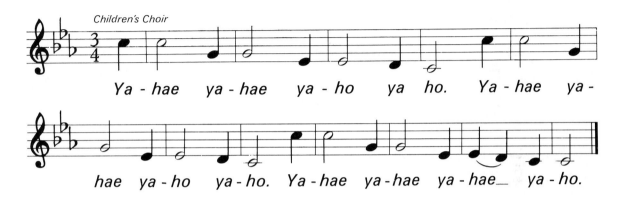

Children's Choir

Ya - hae   ya - hae   ya - ho   ya   ho.   Ya - hae   ya -

hae   ya - ho   ya - ho.   Ya - hae   ya - hae   ya - hae___   ya - ho.

FIRST READER

The East Wind heard their song. He was pleased
and flattered by it. He came back and moved
the branches. Iktomi climbed down from the tree.
He ate his supper and went to sleep while
the wind sang a lullaby for him.

People in Hawaii like to sing songs
that tell stories of their ancestors.
One story is about the goddess Pele
and her search for a home.

One day Pele went from island to island
looking for the best place for her new home.
Because Pele was the goddess of the volcano,
she chose Hawaii, an island with
many volcanoes. A crater of a great volcano
became her home.

The words to "Aia o Pele i Hawaii" mean:

Pele has now come to Hawaii, Oh!
And she is living at Maukele, Oh!

Aia o Pele i Hawaii

Hawaiian Chant

Ai - a   la   o   Pe - le   i   Ha - wa - i,   e - a!

Ke ha - a   ma - i   la - i   Ma - u - ke - le,   e - a!

The picture shows a wood carving of Pele. It is made of wood and real hair. Of what are the eyes made? What makes the Goddess look as though she were ready to dance to an Hawaiian chant?

215

Tall tales in music

"The Greedy Cat" is a tall tale from Russia. A composer has turned the tale into a musical play. Your class should choose a reader and then divide into two groups.

People like to make up stories and songs about things that could never happen. Around the world people tell tales about mighty heroes who could do impossible things. They also tell tales about magic and about witches and elves.

216

The Greedy Cat
A Russian Tale

Music by Carroll Rinehart

READER

Once upon a time there was a Greedy Cat. Her master could no longer afford to feed her. She would have to go out into the world and find her own food. Before she started out, her master gave her a last bowl of porridge and a dish of fat.

ALL

NOW WHAT DO YOU THINK OF THAT?

READER

The Greedy Cat with the enormous appetite gobbled up the food, jumped through the window and ran away. She ran until she came to a farmer.

(Sing "The Greedy Cat Song," verse 1, page 218)

217

The Greedy Cat Song

Group I F   C7   Group II

1. "Good day, Mis-ter Far-mer,"
2. "Good day, Miss_ Dai-sy," } said the Cat, "Good day, Miss Kit-ty,
3. "Good day, good_ sir,"_

F   Group I   C7   F

have you eat - en   yet?" "A lit - tle, but I'm 'most star - ving!

C7
※ sing on v.1

I had a bowl of por-ridge and a dish of fat.

F   C7   F   Bb

Now   that you've men-tioned it,   I'm   not   through,

C7   F

I   think   that   I   will   gob - ble   you!"

C7
※ sing on v. 2

dish   of   fat,   and a   far - - mer.

C7
※ sing on v. 3

dish   of   fat,   and a   far - - mer, and a   cow.

READER

So the Greedy Cat with the ENORMOUS APPETITE opened her mouth and with one big gulp swallowed the farmer.

ALL

NOW WHAT DO YOU THINK OF THAT?

READER

Then she went into the barn. There stood Miss Daisy, the cow.

ALL

OH, NO!   NOT THE COW!

(Sing "The Greedy Cat Song," verse 2)

READER

So the Greedy Cat with the ENORMOUS APPETITE opened her mouth and with one big gulp swallowed the cow.

ALL

NOW WHAT DO YOU THINK OF THAT?

READER

The Greedy Cat started off down the road. Soon she met an old man riding on a donkey.

ALL

THIS CAN NEVER HAPPEN!

(Sing "The Greedy Cat Song," verse 3)

READER

So the Greedy Cat with the ENORMOUS APPETITE opened her mouth very wide and with one huge gulp swallowed the old man and his donkey.

ALL

NOW WHAT DO YOU THINK OF THAT?

The Greedy Cat Song

Group I   F   C7   Group II

4. "Good day, your Ma-jes-ty," said the Cat. "Good day, Miss Kit-ty,
5. "Good day, Miss Mous - ie,"

F   Group I   C7   F

have you eat - en   yet?" "A lit - tle, but I'm 'most star - ving!

C7

I had a bowl of porridge and a dish of fat, a farmer and a cow,

1.
and a man on a don - key.

2.
man on a don-key, a

King on his el - e-phant, and all his men. Now that you've

mentioned it, I'm not through, I think that I will gob-ble you!"

221

READER

The Greedy Cat walked on until she met a King
riding on an elephant, followed by a WHOLE ARMY
OF MEN.

ALL

OH, MY!

(Sing "The Greedy Cat Song," verse 4)

READER

So the Greedy Cat with the ENORMOUS APPETITE
opened her mouth as wide as it would go, and with
one GREAT, HUGE, ENORMOUS GULP swallowed
the King, his elephant, and the WHOLE ARMY
OF MEN.

ALL

NOW WHAT DO YOU THINK OF THAT?

READER

The Greedy Cat moved more slowly now.
She was thinking about taking a nap when she spied
Miss Mousie Bright-Eyes.

ALL

(*Make up something to say here.*)

(Sing "The Greedy Cat Song," verse 5)

READER

So the Greedy Cat with the ENORMOUS APPETITE
opened her mouth a wee, wee bit and swallowed
the little mouse.

ALL

(*whispering*)   Now what do you think of that?

READER

Then the Greedy Cat curled up to go to sleep.

She curled her-self in-to a ball

with the mouse, the el-e-phant, don-key and all

with-in her stom-ach **stretched** out wide,

And those with-in wished they were out-side.

223

Miss Mousie Bright-Eyes looked around inside and
saw the King trying to keep the elephant from
stepping on the soldiers, the soldiers trying to march
in a parade, the man riding the donkey, and the
farmer looking bewildered.

So while the Greedy Cat slept, Miss Mousie
went right to work. She gnawed and gnawed.
She tried and tried until she made a great hole
in the cat's side.

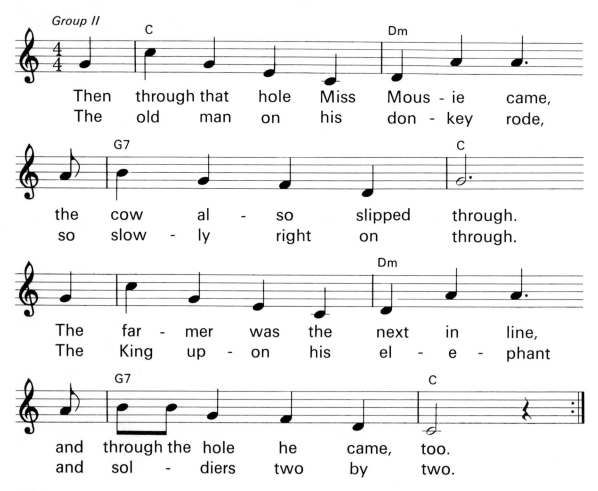

Then through that hole Miss Mous - ie came,
The old man on his don - key rode,

the cow al - so slipped through.
so slow - ly right on through.

The far - mer was the next in line,
The King up - on his el - e - phant

and through the hole he came, too.
and sol - diers two by two.

AND WHAT DO YOU THINK HAPPENED?

READER
Each went his own way, but the Greedy Cat with the
ENORMOUS APPETITE had to spend the rest of the
day looking for a tailor to sew up the hole in her coat.

All · F

There was a Greed-y Cat, SO BIG!

C7

Who had an ap - pe - tite, SO BIG!

C7

Her Mas - ter could-n't feed her, TOO BAD!

C7 · F

She had to find a tai - lor, SO SAD!

ALL
NOW WHAT DO YOU THINK OF THAT?

Beauty and the Beast
Maurice Ravel

Magical tales are often told in music.
"The Greedy Cat" was told with words
and music, so the story was easy to follow.
Sometimes composers do not use words to tell
their tales. They use only music.

Maurice Ravel wrote a suite called *Mother Goose.*
Remember that a suite is a group of pieces.
Each piece in *Mother Goose* tells a part of
a story.

One of the stories Ravel chose was
"Beauty and the Beast." Beauty was
a lovely young lady. One day she
had a conversation with an ugly Beast,
who was really a handsome Prince.

226

Beauty felt sorry for the Beast and
did not want him to die. Because
of her kindness, the spell was broken.
The Beast turned back into a Prince.
Beauty and the Prince married and lived
happily ever after.

Ravel chose a clarinet to play the voice
of Beauty. He chose a bassoon to play
the part of the Beast. When you listen
to the music, find the place
where the wicked spell is broken.

Listen for the music that tells you
the Beast has changed into a Prince.
What instrument is used for the sound
of this magic?

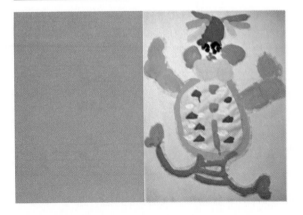

Paint a picture of something that you have imagined. You could draw the Greedy Cat, the ugly Beast, or another strange creature. Make arms that swing, tiny feet, big green ears, or anything else that you can imagine. Use many different colors. This painting of a make-believe creature was done by a third grader.

People sometimes have fun making up
rhymes from words that begin
with the same sound. Here is one about
a fly and a flea.

You can play the bells as you sing
this song. Play the first tone of each measure
on the bells.

A Fly and a Flea

Music by Elie Siegmeister
Traditional Words

228

*A flue is a chimney-pipe.

Music for all the year

Thirty days hath September,
April, June, and November;
February has twenty-eight alone.
All the rest have thirty-one,
Excepting leap year — that's the time
When February's days are twenty-nine.

Anonymous

Patriotic songs

Many songs have been written about
the greatness of our country. These songs
are called **patriotic songs**.

America, the Beautiful

Music by Samuel A. Ward
Words by Katherine Lee Bates

O beau-ti-ful for spa-cious skies, For am-ber waves of grain,

For pur-ple moun-tain maj-es-ties, A-bove the fruit-ed plain,

A-mer-i-ca! A-mer-i-ca! God shed his grace on thee,

A-mer-i-ca! A-mer-i-ca!

And crown thy good with broth-er-hood, From sea to shin-ing sea.

And crown thy good From sea to shin-ing sea.

The harmony part of "America,
the Beautiful" uses only three different pitches.
Play these pitches on the bells.

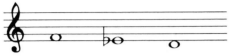

Learn to play the harmony part on the bells.
Learn to sing it. When you know
the harmony part well, sing it with the melody.

Before there were cameras, artists painted pictures about important events. Today, photographers take pictures of important events.

This picture shows the signing of the Declaration of Independence. This event is celebrated every year on July 4.

"The Star-Spangled Banner,"
our **national anthem,** tells about our flag.
Our national anthem and our flag
make us proud of the United States.

The Star-Spangled Banner

Composer Unknown
Words by Francis Scott Key

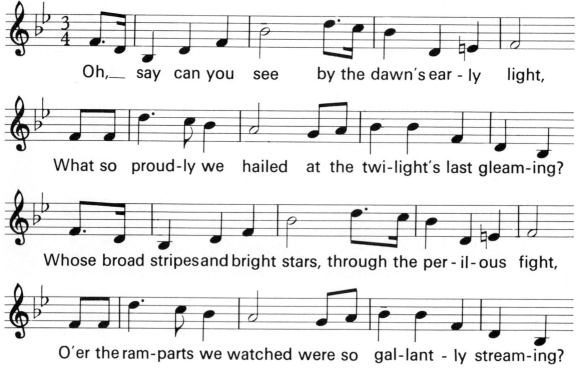

Oh,__ say can you   see   by the dawn's ear - ly   light,

What so   proud-ly we   hailed   at the twi-light's last gleam-ing?

Whose broad stripes and bright stars, through the per - il - ous   fight,

O'er the ram-parts we watched were so   gal-lant - ly   stream-ing?

And the rock-et's red glare, the bombs burst-ing in air,

Gave proof through the night that our flag was still there.

Oh, say does that star-span-gled ban-ner yet wave

O'er the land of the free and the home of the brave?

233

America

Music by Henry Carey
Words by Samuel F. Smith

1. My coun-try, 'tis of thee, Sweet land of lib - er - ty,
2. Our fa - thers' God, to Thee, Au - thor of lib - er - ty,

Of thee I sing;
To Thee we sing;

Land where my fa - thers died, Land of the Pil - grims' pride,
Long may our land be bright. With Free-dom's ho - ly light;

From ev - 'ry— moun-tain-side Let— free - dom ring.
Pro - tect— us— by Thy might, Great God, our King!

Make a painting about autumn.
Will the colors be warm or cool?
Will the day be sunny or cloudy?

How do you want your picture to
look? Will it look happy or sad?
Will it look busy or quiet?

Songs for fall

In the autumn the leaves turn to colors of bright gold and red. The wind sweeps the leaves from the trees and carries them away.

The sounds of autumn are different from those of summer. How would you describe the sound of this melody?

Autumn

Traditional

1. With-ered leaves are fall - ing,   Mourn-ful crows are
2. Hear the wind com- plain - ing,   All the day it's

call - ing,   Days are growing short,_ For the au - tumn's here.
rain - ing,   Sit a-round the fire___ If you wish good cheer.

The melody of "Autumn" moves up and down the scale.
You can play this melody on the bells. Use these bells.

On Halloween

Words and music by Richard Webster

1. It's Hal - low - een when wit - ches fly
2. It's Hal - low - een when ghosts creep in,

in great black streaks a - cross the sky,
Their bod - ies white, both out and in,

And all you hear is one long cry
They all come back to haunt their kin

On Hal - low - een!
On Hal - low - een!

3. It's Halloween when skeletons dance,
Their bones all rattling as they prance.
To move this night's their only chance,
On Halloween.

4. It's Halloween when great black cats
Screech in the night. And flying bats
Perch high upon the witches' hats
On Halloween.

236

Eskimo children celebrate Halloween,
but their ghosts and goblins have
different names. Here is a Halloween song
composed by some Alaskan boys and girls.

If you will play the first tone
in each measure, you will find
a melody pattern. How many times
do you find the pattern?

I-lu-vi-vik

Music by D. Gullickson
Words by L. Felder, L. Leavitt,
G. Okakok, and D. Gullickson

I - lu - vi - vik is a scar - y place, where ghosts and gob-lins

like to race, The In - u - ko-shlim up in the sky, will
when you see___ Kin-u-ia - ki you'd

grab you if you wan-der by. So
bet-ter run home as   quick as can be, 'Cause

In - u - ko-shlim up in the sky, will grab you if you wan-der by.

The National Gallery, London.

238

Artists sometimes show a person being thankful for what he has. This painting was made over 400 years ago. Notice how the head and hands are placed. How does this tell you that the person is giving thanks?

Thanksgiving Day is set aside
as a special time. Nearly everybody
in the world has a day of thanksgiving.
And nearly everybody in the world
sings songs of thanksgiving.

This Thanksgiving song is one which
has been sung in Germany for many years.

Thanksgiving Hymn

German Chorale
Words by Mary Maltbie

Fa-ther in Heav-en whose kind-ness and mer-cy have led us.

Un-der whose gui-dance this boun-ti-ful har-vest has fed us.

Thy prais-es ring as of Thy boun-ty we sing,

Fa-ther, we of-fer thanks-giv-ing.

239

What's a "Turkey Date"?

Make up a musical introduction from the words: "Gobble, gobble, gobble, gobble glee."

Turkey Date

Words and music by Sue Lee

1. Tom Tur - key struts a - round all day,
2. But just you wait, on Tur - key Date

He thinks he's such great stuff.
We'll sure - ly call his bluff.

He spreads his tail, and sings his song,
The on - ly song you'll hear that day

a "Gob - ble, gob - ble, gob - ble, gob - ble glee!"
is a "Gob - ble, gob - ble, gob - ble" from___ me!

Songs for winter

"The First Snow" tells you
what a little girl was thinking
while she watched the snowflakes drift down.

Play the autoharp slowly. Strum forward
and backward to make a harp-like accompaniment.

The First Snow

Music by Clella Lester Perkins
Words by Eleanor Jewett

1. Some-times the clouds are hung a-long
2. And when she wrings the wa-ter out,

the clothes-line of the sky,
Some-times she makes mis-takes.

Like skirts and shirts that Moth-er Goose
And lets the soap chips tum-ble through,

has washed and hung to dry.
In great, soft shi-ny flakes.

Hanukah is a Jewish holiday also called
"The Festival of Lights." Hanukah is
a time for giving gifts, singing, and dancing.

Hanukah Is Here

Words and music by Alan Mills

1. Han-u - kah, Han-u - kah, Han-u - kah is here.
2. Han-u - kah, Han-u - kah, Han-u - kah has come.

Han - u - kah, Han-u - kah, wel-come with good cheer!
Han - u - kah, Han-u - kah, is the time for fun.

Young and old their gifts are bring-ing, Hear their joy - ful
Can - dles glow on the Men - o - rah, As we sing and

voi - ces sing-ing, } For the Feast of Han - u - kah's the
dance the ho - ra,

gay - est time of year! year!

One of the stained glass windows depicting the Twelve Tribes of Israel created by Marc Chagall for the Synagogue at the Hadassah-Hebrew University Medical Center in Jerusalem, Israel. Photograph by Sandak Inc., New York.

This is one of the twelve windows in a new synagogue in Jerusalem. These windows were designed by Marc Chagall. The light coming through the windows makes the colors glow.

You can make a picture that glows when placed to the light.

1. Cut many different shapes out of colored tissue paper.

2. Place the shapes on a sheet of waxed paper. Use liquid starch to paste them down if they move.

3. Put another sheet of waxed paper over the first piece.

4. Press the two pieces together with a hot iron.

5. Tape your picture to a window. How does the color change when you place it on a window?

243

At Christmas time, carols are sung
all over the world. This carol
tells of a home about to be decorated
for Christmas. Everyone is happy and excited.

Deck the Halls

Welsh Folk Carol
Traditional Words

Deck the halls with boughs of hol - ly,
'Tis the sea - son to be jol - ly,

Fa la la la la, la la la la.

Don we now our gay ap - par - el,

Fa___ la la___ la, la la la,

Troll the an - cient Yule - tide car - ol,

Fa la la la la, la la la la.

"Lullaby Carol" is from Poland. Play the finger cymbals at the end of each phrase.

Lullaby Carol

Polish Folk Song
Words Adapted

Lul - la - by, lit - tle one, stars watch-ing— o'er you.

Lul - la - by, lit - tle one, stars watch a - bove.

Lul - la - by,— lit - tle— one, Dear ba - by sleep-ing,

Ma - ry— is hold-ing you, Guard-ing and keep-ing.

Here is an ostinato for the bells.
Play it as an introduction. Then play it
with the song as you sing. Play one note
of the ostinato on the first count
of each measure.

This is a counting song for Christmas.
The numbers help tell the story.

Little Bitty Baby

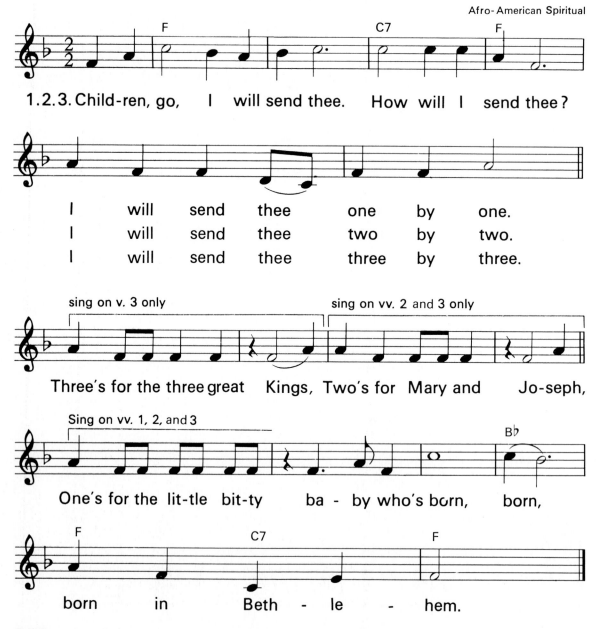

Afro-American Spiritual

1.2.3. Child-ren, go, I will send thee. How will I send thee?

I will send thee one by one.
I will send thee two by two.
I will send thee three by three.

sing on v. 3 only   sing on vv. 2 and 3 only

Three's for the three great Kings, Two's for Mary and Jo-seph,

Sing on vv. 1, 2, and 3

One's for the lit-tle bit-ty ba - by who's born, born,

born in Beth - le - hem.

This Christmas song has been sung for many, many years. The song was first sung in Latin.

O Come, All Ye Faithful

Wade's Cantus Diversi
Translation by Frederick Oakeley

O come, all ye faith-ful, Joy-ful and tri-um-phant,
A - des - te fi - del - es, Lae-ti tri-um-phant-es,

O come ye, O come_ ye to Beth - le - hem.
Ve - ni - te, ve - ni - te in Beth - le - hem.

Come and be - hold Him, Born the King of An - gels,
Na - tum vi - de - te Re - gem an - ge - lo - rum.

O come, let us a - dore Him, O come, let us a - dore Him,
Ve - ni - te, a - do - ra - mus, ve - ni - te a - do - ra - mus,

O come, let us a - dore Him,_ Christ_ the Lord.
Ve - ni - te a - do - ra - mus_ Do - mi - num.

This is a song for the New Year.

I Saw Three Ships

Old Song

1. I saw three ships come sail - ing by,
2. And what do you think was in them then?

sail - ing by, sail - ing by,
In_____ them then? In_____ them then?

I saw three ships come sail - ing by
And what do you think was in them then

On New_____ Year's Day in the morn - ing.
On New_____ Year's Day in the morn - ing.

3. Three pretty girls were in them then,
in them then, in them then.
Three pretty girls were in them then,
On New Year's Day in the morning.

4. And one could whistle and one could sing,
one could sing, one could sing,
And one could whistle and one could sing,
the other play on the violin.

248

The Flag Goes By

Hats off! Hats off!
Along the street there comes
A blare of bugles, a ruffle of drums,
A flash of color beneath the sky:
Hats off! Hats off! The flag is passing by.

Henry Holcomb Bennett

 *The Washington Post*
John Philip Sousa

   John Philip Sousa was the conductor
of the United States Marine Band. He wrote
many marches for this band.
"The Washington Post" is often heard
in parades and in band concerts.

   Listen to the percussion instruments
in this march. Name the ones you recognize.
Notice how the cymbal crashes add
to the excitement of the music.
What other percussion instruments
do you recognize? What makes the music
sound exciting?

I like valentines! All kinds of valentines! Do you?

I Like Valentines

Words and music by Curtis Lee

I like val-en-tines! All kinds of val-en-tines! Lit-tle ti-ny small ones,

great big, tall ones. I like val - en - tines!_____

A val-en-tine made of lace is fine if it's for a pret-ty girl.

But I'd like a big one made with choc-'late can - dy,

D.C. al Fine

I think it's dan - dy to get a val - en - tine.

Do you know what a leprechaun is?
St. Patrick's Day is filled with tales
of leprechauns, mischief,
and Irish songs.

The Leprechaun

Irish Melody
Arranged by Philip Gorden

In a sha - dy nook one moon-light night, a lep - re-chaun I

spied___ with scar - let cap and coat of green, a

knap - sack by his side;___ 'Twas tick - tack-tick his

ham-mer went up-on a ween-y shoe, and I laughed to think of a

purse of gold; but the fair - y was laugh - ing too.___

Let's Go Fly a Kite

Music by Richard M. Sherman
Words by Robert B. Sherman

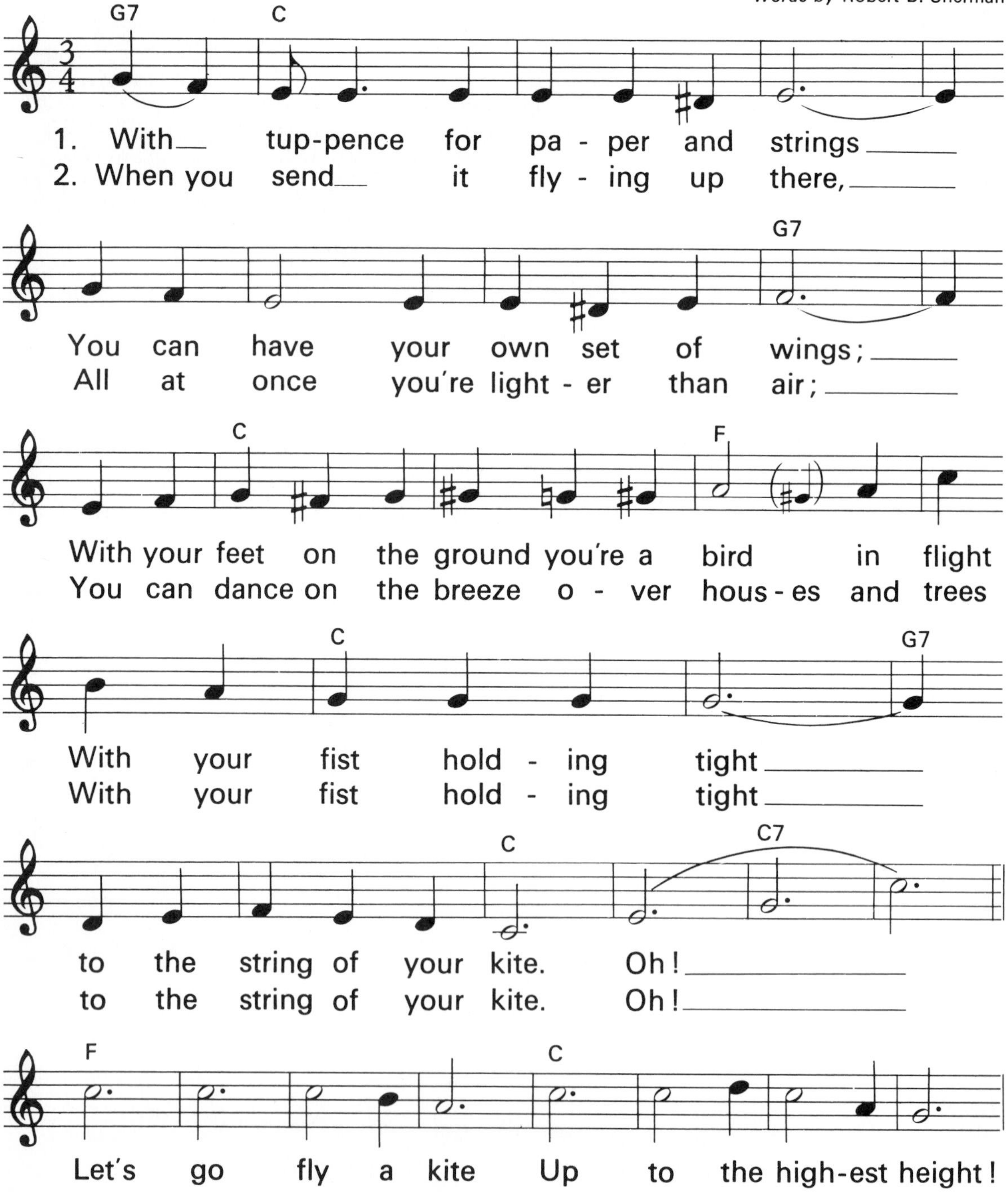
G7 C
1. With tup-pence for pa - per and strings
2. When you send it fly - ing up there,
G7
You can have your own set of wings;
All at once you're light - er than air;
C F
With your feet on the ground you're a bird in flight
You can dance on the breeze o - ver hous - es and trees
C G7
With your fist hold - ing tight
With your fist hold - ing tight
C C7
to the string of your kite. Oh!
to the string of your kite. Oh!
F C
Let's go fly a kite Up to the high-est height!

Let's go fly a kite And send it soar - ing

Up through the at - mos-phere, Up where the air is clear.

Oh, let's go fly a kite!

Kite Days

A kite, a sky, and a good firm breeze,
And acres of ground away from the trees,
And one hundred yards of clean, strong string
O boy, O boy! I call that Spring!

Mark Sawyer

Think about the colors of spring. Think about what spring means to you. Do you feel different in spring than you do in winter? Paint a picture that tells your classmates how you feel about spring.

The month of June brings thoughts
of swimming and taking trips away from home.
What do you like to do during your vacation?

You're On Vacation Time

Words and music by Michael Stevens

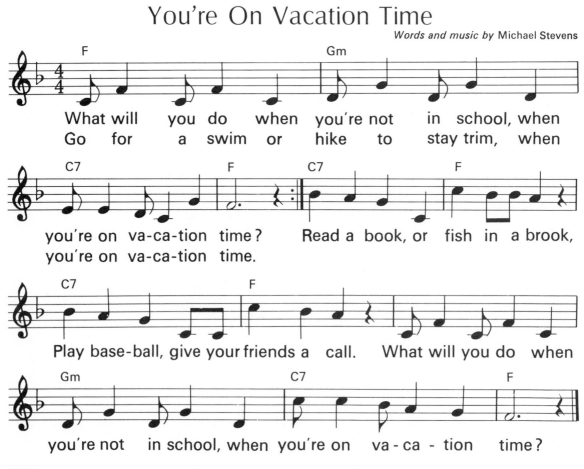

What will you do when you're not in school, when
Go for a swim or hike to stay trim, when

you're on va-ca-tion time? Read a book, or fish in a brook,
you're on va-ca-tion time.

Play base-ball, give your friends a call. What will you do when

you're not in school, when you're on va-ca-tion time?

254

GLOSSARY OF TERMS

accent—a strong sound in music, **97**

alto—a woman's low voice, **18**

autoharp—a stringed instrument played by pressing a bar with one hand and strumming with the other hand, **51**

ballet—a story told through dance and music, **121**

bar—a line by which notes are divided into groups on the staff, **105**

bass—a man's low voice, **18**

bassoon—a woodwind instrument played by blowing air through a double reed. It is longer than the oboe and plays pitches much lower than the oboe, **56**

castanets—percussion instruments made of wood and played by shaking or striking, **28**

chantey—a solo-response song sung by sailors, **11**

chord—the result of tones being played together, **31**

chorus—a singing group, **10**

composing—making up a piece of music, **83**

conductor—the leader of a group of musical performers, **94**

descant—a second melody part of a song that is sung above or below the melody of a song, **16**

double reed—a part of the bassoon and oboe through which air is blown, **56**

duet—two voices or instruments used together, **20**

eighth note—a short sound in music, **85**

fanfare—a musical way of saying something is about to happen, **62**

flat—a symbol that indicates the pitch of a note is to be lowered one half-step, **14**

form—the plan by which music is put together, **180**

forte—loud, **139**

half note—a long sound in music which is twice as long as the sound of a quarter note, **91**

harmony—two or more tones being sung or played together, **129**

imitation—music played by one voice or instrument and echoed by another, **176**

improvising—making up music while performing, **195**

keyboard—the black and white keys of a piano, organ, or harpsichord, **48**

measure—a grouping of notes divided by bars, **105**

melody—high and low tones sounding one after the other, **112**

meter signature—the two numbers at the beginning of each song which tell how many counts are in each measure and the note which gets one count, **107**

national anthem—the national song of a country, **230**

oboe—a woodwind instrument played by blowing air through a double reed, **56**

octave—the eighth full tone above or below a given tone, **114**

opera—a story told by singing and the playing of instruments, **64**

original instruments—objects that are found or made which are used as musical instruments, **40**

ostinato—a repeated pattern used to accompany a song, **45**

patriotic songs—songs about one's country, **230**

patterns—the way in which tones of a melody are grouped, **124, 146**

percussion instrument—a musical instrument played by shaking or striking, **21**

phrase—a part of a longer melody, **156**

piano—a large keyboard instrument played by pressing the keys, **48**

pick-up notes—notes in an incomplete first measure of a piece. When combined with the notes of the last measure, which is also incomplete, they make a complete measure, **111**

pitch—the highness or lowness of a tone, **42**

quarter note—a long sound in music which is twice as long as the sound of an eighth note, **89**

quarter rest—a place in a song where one does not sing or play and which lasts as long as a quarter note, **89**

repeated tones—the same tone sounded many times, **112**

resonator bells—tuned percussion instruments played by striking with a mallet, **44**

rest—a place in a song where one does not sing or play, **89**

rhythm—the movement of long and short sounds in music, **80**

rhythm pattern—a group of long and short sounds, **149**

round—a melody sung by two or more groups starting at different times, **14**

scale—a series of tones arranged in a special order, **119**

sharp—a symbol that indicates the pitch of a note is to be raised one half-step, **108**

slide—the part of the trombone that is moved to change the pitch, **59**

slide trombone—same as trombone, **59**

solo—a melody sung or played by one person, **10**

solo response—one person sings alone and other voices answer, **10**

soprano—a woman's high voice, **18**

staff—the lines and spaces on which music is written, **115**

suite—a group of short pieces of music, **194**

tempo—the speed of music, **138**

tenor—a man's high voice, **18**

tie—a mark which connects two notes of the same pitch, **166**

timbre—the special sound of each voice or instrument, **17**

triangle—a percussion instrument made of metal and played by striking with a metal rod, **34**

trombone—a brass instrument played by blowing air into a mouthpiece and moving the slide, **59**

variation—a melody played in a different way, **191**

viola—a four-stringed instrument shaped like a violin but slightly

256

larger in size. It is played with a bow and has a rich, mellow sound, **52**

volume—the loudness or softness of music, **139**

whole note—a long sound in music, **84**

woodwind family—a group of musical instruments including the bassoon, oboe, clarinet, and flute, **56**

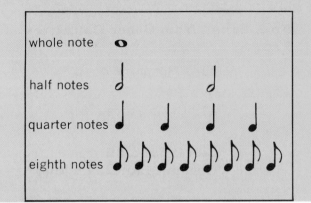

whole note

half notes

quarter notes

eighth notes

CLASSIFIED INDEX

257

Folk Songs from Other Countries

Foreign-Language Songs

LISTENING SELECTIONS

ALPHABETICAL SONG INDEX

(Continued from page IV.)

Schroder Music Company for "Jenney Appleseed" © Copyright 1964 by Schroder Music Company care of Larry Shayne Music, Inc., Hollywood, California. Used by permission. All rights reserved.

Shawnee Press, Inc. for "The Goat" collected and adapted by Rudolph Goehr, words by Leo Israel, arr. by Hawley Ades; "Hans of Schnocheloch" and "One Day My Mother Went to Market" from LITTLE FOLK SONGS by Leo Israel and Rudolph Goehr; "Mi Burro," words by Harriet Barnett, music by Betty M. Barlow from "Hola!" (Vamos a cantar).

Stormking Music, Inc. for "Dansons la Capucine" from FAVORITE FRENCH FOLK SONGS translated and adapted by Alan Mills. © Copyright 1963 Stormking Music, Inc. All rights reserved. International Copyright Secured. Used by permission.

Janet Tobitt for "Kookaburra" by Marion Sinclair from THE DITTY BAG. Reprinted by permission.

Charles E. Tuttle Co., Inc., for "Aia A Pele i Hawaii" from HAWAII: MUSIC IN ITS HISTORY, by Ruth Hausman. Used by permission.

Ruth Waller and the Arizona State Department of Public Instruction for "Night Song" by Elizabeth Lee Waller. Reprinted by permission.

Walton Music Company for "The Leprechaun" from SONGS OF MAN by Luboff and Stracke, copyright 1959. Used by permission.

Frederick Warne & Co., Ltd. for "I Saw Three Ships" from THE BABY'S OPERA by Walter Crane. Used by permission.

Western Publishing Company, Inc. for "Kite Days" by Mark Sawyer, copyright 1939, copyright renewed 1967 by Story Parade, Inc. Reprinted by permission of Western Publishing Company, Inc.

Do You Know?

1. Which one of these is <u>not</u> a percussion instrument?

   a. castanets   **b.** triangle   **c.** bassoon   **d.** shakers

2. A kind of song that sailors sing when they work together is called

   a. a chantey   **b.** an opera   **c.** a round   **d.** a carol

3. There are four instruments in a string quartet. They are two violins, a viola, and

   .a clarinet   a cello   a trombone

4. Listen to the recording of "Never in Our Mountains." Is the first voice you hear a soprano or a tenor?

5. Here are some musical notes.

   Arrange them in order from the shortest to the longest.

6. Look at this music.

   The meter signature is $\frac{2}{4}$. The top number tells you that each measure has two counts. The bottom number tells you the kind of note that gets one count. In this music, the kind of note that gets one count is a

   a. half note   **b.** whole note   **c.** quarter note

7. Look at the music in Question 6. What is the pitch name of the first note? Of the last note?

8. Clap this rhythm pattern.

$\frac{2}{2}$ — — — — | — — — — | — — — — | — — — γ

Which of these songs uses this rhythm pattern?

   a. Little Jack Horner   **b.** Mi Burro
   c. Supercalifragilisticexpialidocious

9. Clap this rhythm pattern.

$\frac{3}{4}$ ♩ ♩ ♩ | ♩. ♪ ♪ | ♩ ♩ ♩ | ♩. ♪ ♪ | ♩ ♩ ♩ | ♩. |

Which of these songs uses this rhythm pattern?

a. America   **b.** Yankee Doodle   **c.** Jingle Bells

10. Listen to the recording of "For Health and Strength" or sing this song. Which of these arrows shows how the melody of the words "For health and strength" moves?

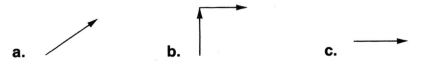

   a.   **b.**   **c.**

11. Here is part of the music from two songs.

Which music moves by skips? Which music moves by steps? Play the songs on the bells and sing them.

12. This sign p ———— f ———— p tells you something about how loud or soft the music should sound. It tells you that the music should

   a. start loud, then get soft, then get loud again.
   b. start soft, get loud, then get soft again.
   c. start loud then get soft near the end.

13. The song "Fiddle-Dee-Dee" has this melody pattern.

   Listen to the recording of this song. How many times do you hear this melody pattern?

   a. once   **b.** twice
          c. four times

14. Some music is in A B A form. In this form of music, if the first part of a piece sounds like a march, and the second part sounds like a dance, then the third part will

   a. sound like a march.
   b. sound like a dance.
   c. sound like a storm.

15. Here is the beginning of the C scale. Fill in other notes of the C scale and label each one.

C

Who Am I?

1. I look like a long wooden pipe and I have a very deep voice. I have cousins who also make music. We all sing when someone blows into us through two thin pieces of reed.

2. I began life as a steel bar, but now I am bent into a three-sided shape. My voice is not loud, but when I sound like a ringing bell, I can be heard over even the loudest orchestra.

3. I have the same name as some girls. Like my cousins, I have strings and a bow. One of my cousins is smaller than I am and is much more popular. Even one of my larger cousins, whose voice is deeper than mine, gets more of a chance to sing solos than I do.

4. I like to play in bands and orchestras. I am different from my friends because I have no keys to push or holes to cover or strings to play. I have a slide that goes in and out, and this is how I change my voice from low to high and high to low.

5. I can't play a tune but I make sounds like "click" and "clack," and people like to use me when they dance—especially in Spain and Mexico. I'm even used sometimes in big orchestras. From my name you can tell that I look like a chestnut shell.

6. I can sound more tones than any other instrument. This is one reason why more people play me than any other instrument. I come in several different sizes and shapes. My name is a musical term that means soft, but I can also sound loud.

Games and Puzzles

A MUSICAL MYSTERY

This story has some mystery words. Only a person who knows music notes can read them. Can you figure out the mystery words?

One day [♪ notes] the bird was very hungry.

He hopped over to Mr. Jones's [♪ notes]

patch and began to [♪ notes] . Just then, Mr.

Jones came around the corner and saw [♪ notes] .

Quick as a wink, he threw a net over [♪ notes]

and took him over to the bird [♪ notes] . "You'll

never eat my [♪ notes] again," said Mr.

Jones. Poor [♪ notes] begged, "Oh, please —

won't anybody help me?" Billy the [♪ notes]

saw what had happened. Just as Mr. Jones opened

the [♪ notes] door, Billy stung him on the hand.

Mr. Jones yelled and let go of [♪ notes] who

267

quickly hopped out of sight. Billy buzzed happily,

and went home to tell his 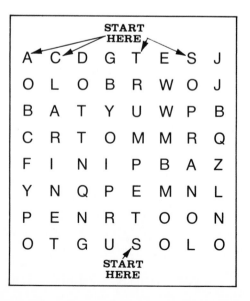 what he had

done.

SCRAMBLED NOTES

The words below were written on a funny type-writer. They are names of kinds of notes. What did the typewriter really mean to say?

TRRAUEQ   GITHEH

LOEHW   FLAH

Now write these words as notes.

Make up a list of more scrambled music words for other people. See if you can fool them.

A MUSICAL MAZE

Some music terms are hidden in the maze below. Here is how to find them.

The starting point for each term is marked with an arrow.

Move down, across, or down at a slant. You may only move to a neighboring letter. You must not skip any letters.

START HERE

A	C	D	G	T	E	S	J
O	L	O	B	R	W	O	J
B	A	T	Y	U	W	P	B
C	R	T	O	M	M	R	Q
F	I	N	I	P	B	A	Z
Y	N	Q	P	E	M	N	L
P	E	N	R	T	O	O	N
O	T	G	U	S	O	L	O

START HERE

Dance It Your Way

MOVING TO RHYTHM PATTERNS

You can move to rhythm patterns. Work with a partner. One of you will play patterns on an instrument. The other will dance. Choose an instrument to strike, shake, or scrape.

Play a rhythm pattern for your partner's dance.

Play other patterns for the dance. Put patterns together for a longer dance. Switch parts and try different instruments.

A DANCE FOR "JARABE TAPATIO"

Here is a dance for "Jarabe Tapatio," on page 29. First, listen to the song and sing it. Then learn the dance.

Formation: Make a large circle, with everyone having a partner. All hold hands.

Measures 1-2: Take 3 steps to the center of the circle and bow. The first step is on the word "meet." Start with your right foot.

Measures 3-4: Take 4 steps backward. Start with your left foot.

Measures 5-6: Hook right elbows with your partner and move clockwise around each other.

Measures 7-8: Hook left elbows with your partner and move in the other direction.

Measures 9-10: All join hands and circle right.

Measures 11-12: Circle left. On the word "Ole," clap your hands in the air.

After you have learned this dance, plan a different way to do it.

IN STEP WITH TIME

How many kinds of clocks can you name? Talk about how they look and how they work.

Pretend you are in a big clock shop. There are many kinds of clocks in this shop. Choose one kind of clock you would like to be. Try different ways of showing how your clock works. You might show how to wind it. You might show how it runs down.

You may need to have someone move with you. You also may want to ask someone to make sounds for your clock.

How is your clock like some of the other clocks? How is it different?

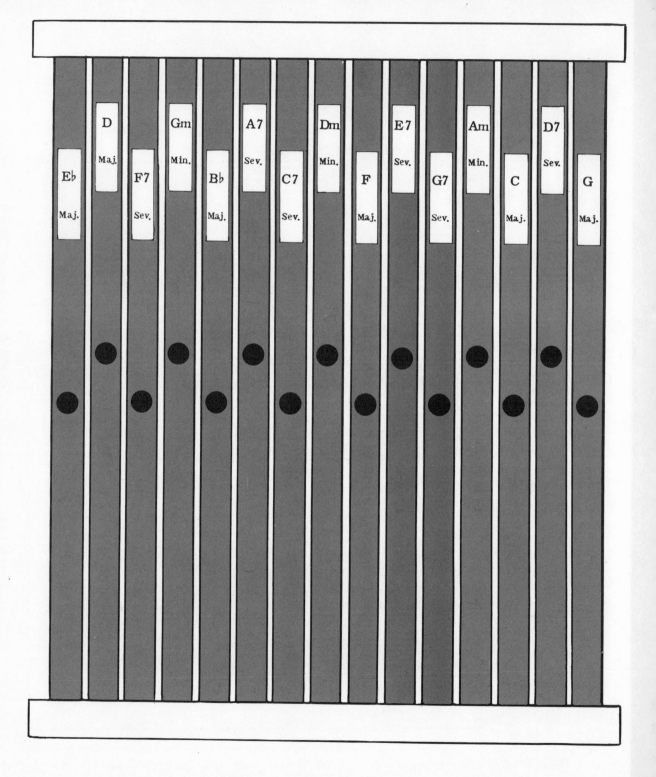